CHRIS PENMAN

The Unseen Green

Debunking Climate Myths, Debating Rising CO2, Defining Eco-Solutions

Copyright © 2024 by Chris Penman

No part of this publication may be reproduced, stored in a retrieval system, or transmitted in any form or by any means, electronic, mechanical, photocopying, recording, or otherwise, without the prior written permission of the publisher.

Published by STARK Consulting Engineers.

This book is designed to provide information on the subjects covered. It is sold with the understanding that the author and publisher are not engaged in rendering professional services in the book. If expert assistance is required, the services of a competent professional should be sought.

Neither the author nor STARK Consulting Engineers shall be liable for any loss of profit or any other commercial damages, including but not limited to special, incidental, consequential, or other damages. The views and opinions expressed in this book are those of the author and do not necessarily reflect the official policy or position of STARK Consulting Engineers. Information in this book is provided on an "as is" basis, with no guarantees of completeness, accuracy, usefulness or timeliness, and without any warranties of any kind whatsoever, express or implied. Readers should not act upon any information provided in this book without seeking professional advice tailored to their individual circumstances.

First edition

*This book was professionally typeset on Reedsy.
Find out more at reedsy.com*

Contents

IMPORTANT - READ THIS FIRST   v
INTRODUCTION   x
1   UNMASKING THE CLIMATE AGENDA   1
  The Politics of Climate Change   1
  Virtue Signalling in Environmental Campaigns   5
  Fear-Mongering Techniques   8
2   THE GREENING EFFECT OF CO_2 14
  Photosynthesis Boost   14
  Revisiting Climate Models   18
  Environmental and Economic Benefits   21
3   THE REALITIES OF RENEWABLE ENERGY   27
  Understanding Renewable Limitations   27
  The Economics of Renewables   30
  Technological Advances and Setbacks   34
4   THE DARK SIDE OF RENEWABLES   41
  Land Use and Biodiversity   41
  Resource Drain and Pollution   44
  Economic Impact   47
5   THE DEPENDENCE ON CONVENTIONAL ENERGY   53
  The Role of Fossil Fuels   53
  Nuclear Energy: A Misunderstood Alternative?   57
  Bridging the Gap   60
6   THE TRUE COST OF RISING FUEL PRICES   67
  Poverty and Inequality   67

Food Security Challenges	70
Alternative Solutions	74
7 THE UNSUNG HERO: NATURAL GAS	80
Natural Gas and Agriculture	80
Economic Advantages	84
Environmental Considerations	87
8 RETHINKING NUCLEAR ENERGY	93
Modern Nuclear Technologies	93
Addressing Public Concerns	97
Nuclear in the Energy Mix	100
9 CLIMATE REPARATIONS AND GLOBAL INEQUALITY	106
The Concept of Climate Reparations	106
Consequences for Developing Nations	110
Crafting Better Policies	113
10 TAKING ACTION: PRACTICAL STEPS FOR THE SCEPTICAL	119
Individual Impact	119
Community Initiatives	123
Policy Advocacy	126
THE FUTURE IS YOURS TO SHAPE	133

IMPORTANT - READ THIS FIRST

Hi, I'm Chris Penman, and I'm grateful you took the opportunity to get this book. My journey into unravelling the complex web of climate change narratives has spanned over three decades. Throughout this time, I've encountered countless misconceptions and unanswered questions which propelled me to author "The Unseen Green: Debunking Climate Myths, Debating Rising CO2, Defining Eco-Solutions."

Having been deeply embedded in the environmental sector, I've realised that the quest for truth in the climate debate is fraught with skewed facts and rampant misinformation. This prompted my resolve to bring clarity and factual integrity to the fore through this much-publicised book.

After all, maybe you've found yourself frustrated, trying to differentiate between scientific fact and political opinion, feeling overwhelmed by the conflicting reports and studies that flood your newsfeed. The complexity of the information available makes it virtually impossible for anyone without a scientific background to feel confident about what to believe.

Maybe you've also felt disillusioned by the doom-laden forecasts that never seem to manifest, which leads to a growing sense of scepticism about all environmental claims. This repeated cycle of alarm followed by anticlimactic reality can leave anyone feeling jaded and distrustful of all sources.

Or maybe you've even tried engaging in discussions or debates, only to find yourself outmatched by seemingly more informed individuals using jargon or referencing studies you've never heard of, making you feel excluded from meaningful dialogue.

The truth is, you're not alone. It seems most are becoming victims of this overwhelming and convoluted narrative that drowns out simple truths and fosters an environment of confusion rather than clarity.

That feeling of helplessness, frustration, or even anger isn't uncommon; it's a shared emotional cocktail that many who seek the truth sip from, standing on the sidelines of science debates, feeling the facts slip through their fingers like sand.

Here's what most don't realise: the larger issue at hand isn't just about understanding the data—it's about reclaiming the narrative from those who use climate discussions as a platform for political gain rather than a genuine concern for environmental stewardship.

And now with the possibility of new policies and technologies emerging at a rapid pace, the urgency to stay informed and critical is greater than ever. Yet, this acceleration also breeds more room for misinformation and confusion, leaving the public caught in a whirlwind of doubt and indecision.

It seems most are left in a state of paralysis by analysis, caught between dire warnings and hopeful assurances, making it extraordinarily difficult to discern where the truth lies and what actions are genuinely necessary for the future of our planet.

The Misinformation Maze

Navigating the intricate web of climate change information can be exasperating, especially when you're committed to uncovering the truth amidst a sea of myths and deceptions. Most seekers of truth, like yourself, find themselves caught in a relentless cycle that I call the Misinformation Maze. This endless loop of confusion and frustration is a common ordeal, and today, we will walk through each of its five tortuous steps, understanding how each phase seamlessly transitions into the next, trapping you in a perpetual cycle of misinformation and despair.

Discovery Dissonance

Perhaps you start with an earnest quest for knowledge. You dive into articles, documentaries, and forums. Initially, everything seems factual, filled with numbers, graphs, and compelling narratives. Yet, the more you delve, the more discrepancies emerge. Some sources claim that climate change is a hoax, while others present a looming catastrophe. This clash of information leaves you bewildered, questioning the credibility of everything you read. This dissonance is the first trap of the Misinformation Maze.

Overwhelm Overload

As you struggle to make sense of the conflicting information, the sheer volume of data becomes overwhelming. Each article leads to ten more, each with its own perspective and array of facts. Maybe you find yourself spending hours, if not days, trying to validate the claims of one source against another. The complexity multiplies, and soon, you are not just confused but also mentally exhausted. This overload is not just about information but also about the emotional toll it takes on you, leaving you too fatigued to question further.

Analysis Paralysis

By now, your initial resolve turns into indecision. Maybe you ponder over the right course of action but feel stuck. Should you change your lifestyle, advocate for policy changes, or perhaps dismiss the issue as unsolvable? Doubt creeps in, freezing you into inaction. You want to make informed decisions, but the conflicting information paralyses you. Each step feels like a misstep, and fear of making the wrong choice looms large, anchoring you in place.

Cynical Retreat

Frustration builds up, leading to disillusionment. Perhaps you start questioning the motives behind the information. Who benefits from the myths? Is every source tainted by bias? This scepticism might seem like a protective shield, but it often morphs into cynicism. You might withdraw, deciding that there's no point in engaging if you can't find unadulterated truth. This retreat might offer a temporary respite from the chaos but ultimately keeps you disengaged from meaningful action or understanding.

False Resolution

Eventually, a semblance of resolution might appear. Maybe you latch onto a source that aligns with your worldview or find a community that supports your perspective. Relief washes over you as you feel grounded in this new belief. However, this resolution is often built on the shaky ground of partial truths and unvetted information. Sooner than you expect, a new piece of evidence or a persuasive argument shakes your foundation, and the cycle begins anew. You are back at the start, facing the same dissonances, overwhelmed yet again by the vast maze of information.

It just goes to show you would be wise to adopt a different approach to navigate through the lies and misinformation surrounding global warming and end this cycle of pain and frustration.

Which is why I'm glad you're reading this book, because as you turn the page and start reading, you will finally discover the insights and answers that you've been seeking.

INTRODUCTION

Imagine a world where the air you breathe is as fresh as the morning dew, where cities are bustling with green technologies, and where each step you take leaves a lighter footprint on the earth. Now, let's step back into reality—a reality where climate change is not just a distant threat, but a present challenge, muddied by myths, misconceptions, and heated debates. What if you could cut through the noise and understand the true nuances of this global issue? What if you could be part of a movement that not only debates but also defines the path forward? This is not just another book on climate change; it's a journey towards clarity and action.

In an age brimming with information overload, it's easy to feel overwhelmed and sceptical about what to believe, especially when it comes to a topic as complex and politicised as climate change. You've likely heard conflicting reports about carbon emissions, seen the debates over the effectiveness of renewable energy, and felt the pinch of rising fuel prices. Amidst this whirlwind of information, it's crucial to find a narrative that resonates with truth, stripped of agenda and bias. This is where "The Unseen Green: Debunking Climate Myths, Debating Rising CO_2, Defining Eco-Solutions" steps in.

Through the pages of this book, you're not just reading another doom-and-gloom climate prophecy or an overly optimistic green utopia. Instead, you're embarking on an evidence-based exploration of the most contentious issues surrounding climate change today. From unmasking the hidden agendas behind global climate talks to delving into the realities and challenges of renewable energy, this book aims to equip you with a holistic understanding of the current climate landscape.

The journey through these pages is structured to challenge the status quo, question mainstream narratives, and offer a fresh perspective on what it means to be environmentally conscious in the 21st century. It's about understanding the role of conventional energy sources, the economic implications of energy policies, and the technological innovations that could lead us into a new era of environmental sustainability.

But why should you care? Because the outcome of this global dialogue will shape the world that you inhabit. It will determine the kind of air you breathe, the type of energy that powers your home, and even the cost of the food on your table. Climate change is not just an environmental issue; it's an economic, social, and personal issue that affects everyone—regardless of where you live or what you believe.

Consider the chapters on the unsung hero of the energy sector: natural gas. While often overshadowed by the more glamorous solar and wind projects, natural gas has played a critical role in reducing carbon emissions by replacing more polluting fuels. Understanding its role in the energy mix is crucial for a balanced view on sustainable practices. Similarly, the discussions on nuclear energy aim to shed light on its potential resurgence as a powerful, clean energy source, despite its controversial past.

Moreover, this book doesn't shy away from the global disparities highlighted by climate change. The chapters on climate reparations and global inequality address how climate policies affect different regions and why a one-size-fits-all approach may not be effective. Recognising these inequalities is the first step towards crafting fair and effective global climate solutions.

Lastly, "Taking Action: Practical Steps for the Sceptical" is perhaps the most crucial part of this exploration. It's easy to feel powerless in the face of such a monumental issue, but this chapter is about transforming concern into action. Whether you're a policymaker, a business owner, or a concerned citizen, you'll find practical steps that can be taken to make a real difference. This isn't about preaching or converting the sceptics; it's about offering tangible, realistic ways to contribute to a healthier planet.

As you turn these pages, keep an open mind. Challenge yourself to see beyond the headlines and the hype. Engage with the data, listen to the expert interviews, and question the world around you. This book isn't just a collection of facts and figures; it's a call to action, a primer for those ready to make informed decisions about their future and the future of our planet.

So, take this knowledge, arm yourself with understanding, and step forward into a world where you can be a part of the solution. The truth isn't just out there; it's right here, in your hands, waiting to be uncovered. Let's begin this journey together.

1

UNMASKING THE CLIMATE AGENDA

"It is difficult to get a man to understand something, when his salary depends upon his not understanding it!" - *Upton Sinclair*

The Politics of Climate Change

Delving into the intricate world of climate change, it's impossible to overlook the magnetic pull of politics that shapes every contour of environmental policy. Whether you're a seasoned eco-warrior or just starting to scratch the surface of ecological issues, understanding the political dimensions is crucial to demystifying the actions and inactions characterising this global challenge.

The Role of Political Agendas in Climate Policy

At the heart of climate policy, political agendas play a pivotal role, often acting as both the propellant and the brake in the legislative and executive processes. Governments worldwide grapple with the balancing act of advancing environmental protections while also catering to their political base and economic interests. This seesaw is not just about choosing between right and wrong but is heavily influenced by the complex interplay of ideology, economic considerations, and public opinion.

For instance, consider the varying environmental policies adopted by different countries. In some nations, you'll find aggressive commitments to renewable energy and strict emissions regulations. These policies often emerge from political parties with a strong environmental plank in their platform, supported by a populace that values sustainability and is aware of the long-term benefits of environmental stewardship.

On the flip side, there are countries where fossil fuel industries hold significant sway over politics. In these places, political agendas may lean towards maintaining the status quo or even rolling back existing environmental protections. This stance isn't just about a lack of will but a calculated political move to support economic sectors that are perceived as vital for the country's immediate economic interests and are major employers.

Analysis of Policy-Making Processes

Understanding the policy-making process is akin to watching a game of chess. It's strategic, often convoluted, and always aimed at a longer-term agenda. The creation of climate policy is no exception and can be seen as a multi-stage process involving various stakeholders, including politicians, scientists, businesses, and civil society.

Initially, the scientific community plays a crucial role by providing the data and evidence needed to understand the environmental challenges at hand. This information, however, must be translated into actionable policies, which is where the role of political judgement comes into play. Politicians must decide how to incorporate scientific findings into laws and regulations that are practical, sustainable, and, critically, palatable to their constituents.

During this process, public opinion can significantly sway the direction and ambition of policy-making. In democracies especially, where politicians' primary goal is re-election, strong public support for environmental issues can lead to more robust and ambitious climate policies. Conversely, if the electorate is indifferent or hostile to environmental regulations, politicians may find it expedient to dilute or delay necessary measures.

The Impact of Lobbying in Climate Legislation

Lobbying is a powerful tool that can be used to both advance and obstruct climate legislation. Various interest groups, from environmental NGOs to fossil fuel companies, spend considerable resources to influence politicians and sway public opinion to align with their interests.

For example, environmental groups lobby for stricter regulations on emissions and higher investments in renewable energy. They bring to the table not just moral arguments but economic data and success stories from around the globe to show the feasibility and benefits of such measures.

Contrastingly, industries that might incur costs due to stringent environmental laws, such as the oil, gas, and coal sectors, also engage in intense lobbying efforts. Their goal is often to delay or weaken legislation, emphasise the economic risks of strong environmental laws, and advocate for slower transitions to alternative energy sources.

This tug of war in lobbying creates a dynamic battleground where the future of climate policy is shaped. The outcomes of these battles are crucial, as they determine how effectively a country can respond to environmental challenges and contribute to global efforts in combating climate change.

In navigating this complex landscape, you, as someone keen on understanding the true dynamics of climate change, must look beyond mere rhetoric. The interplay of political agendas, policy-making processes, and lobbying reveals not just the challenges but also the opportunities for creating effective and sustainable environmental policies. By understanding these forces, you can better appreciate the intricacies of climate change beyond the headlines, helping to foster a more informed and engaged approach to one of the most pressing issues of our time.

Virtue Signalling in Environmental Campaigns

Definition and examples of virtue signalling

Imagine scrolling through your social media feed and stumbling across a post from a well-known multinational proudly announcing its commitment to "going green" by 2030. The company boasts about reducing carbon emissions, using sustainable materials, or perhaps funding a small rainforest preservation project. On the surface, these initiatives might seem like groundbreaking steps towards environmental stewardship. But when you peel back the layers, you might discover that these claims are more about garnering positive public opinion rather than enacting substantial environmental change. This phenomenon is known as virtue signalling.

Virtue signalling occurs when individuals or organisations attempt to project an image of environmental consciousness or moral superiority to enhance their standing among peers or within the public eye, rather than because of a committed belief in environmental action. It's a performative act, often adopted by businesses to align with the prevailing ethical outlook of their consumer base, without necessarily incorporating deep, systemic changes that would result in significant environmental benefits.

For example, a fashion retailer might launch an "eco-friendly" line of clothing, which, upon investigation, reveals only a small percentage of recycled materials while the bulk of their production continues to rely heavily on unsustainable practices and cheap labour. Similarly, an oil company might run an extensive advertising campaign highlighting their investment in renewable energy, which is, in reality, just a drop in the ocean compared to their investment in fossil fuels.

How virtue signalling influences public opinion

The impact of virtue signalling on public opinion is profound and multifaceted. On one hand, it can raise awareness about certain environmental issues. When celebrities or influential companies take a stand on climate change, for instance, their actions can inspire fans and consumers to become more aware of these issues. However, the downside is that this awareness is often shallow and not backed by a deep understanding or commitment to real change.

Moreover, virtue signalling can create a misleading representation of progress. Companies that are excellent at crafting a green public image can lead you to believe that more is being done to combat climate change than is actually the case. This misperception can reduce the urgency among the general public to push for more significant, systemic changes. It can also lead to consumer cynicism; as more people recognise virtue signalling for what it is, they may become sceptical of all corporate environmental claims, potentially dismissing genuine efforts alongside the disingenuous ones.

The influence of virtue signalling extends into consumer behaviour as well. It can shift purchasing decisions, leading individuals to choose one product over another based on perceived environmental benefits, which might not necessarily reflect the true ecological impact of the product. This not only distorts the market but also often diverts attention and resources away from products and services that might offer more substantial environmental benefits.

The consequences of virtue signalling on genuine environmental efforts

Virtue signalling can undermine genuine environmental efforts in several ways. Primarily, it can divert resources—both in terms of money and attention—away from initiatives that could make a real difference. When substantial funds are funnelled into projects that are more about appearances than actual impact, less is available for initiatives with a genuine potential to effect change.

Additionally, the prevalence of virtue signalling can lead to a general erosion of trust. When you're bombarded with messages from companies that claim to be green but are later exposed for environmental malpractice, it's natural to become sceptical of all claims of corporate environmental responsibility. This scepticism can extend to undervaluing or mistrusting legitimate environmental science and activism, potentially hampering efforts to mobilise public support for necessary policy changes or grassroots movements.

Furthermore, virtue signalling can saturate the media with a particular brand of easy, feel-good environmentalism that requires little by way of personal or corporate sacrifice. This can lower the overall expectations of what environmental responsibility should entail, setting a superficial standard that undercuts more profound, challenging, but necessary actions like major reductions in consumption or sweeping changes to production processes.

In summary, while virtue signalling in environmental campaigns can occasionally spark initial interest or awareness regarding climate issues, its broader implications can often hinder more than help. By promoting a superficial form of environmentalism, it not only misleads public perception but also potentially obstructs the pathways to implementing the deep systemic changes that are required to truly address the environmental crises we face.

Fear-Mongering Techniques

Techniques used to instil fear about climate change

Let's dive right in. When you flick through your morning news or scroll your social media feed, you're likely to encounter dramatic headlines about the imminent doom of our planet due to climate change. These aren't just random alarm bells; they are meticulously crafted messages. One common technique is the use of catastrophic language. Terms like 'apocalyptic,' 'disaster,' and 'irreversible damage' are frequently employed to grab your attention and evoke a high emotional response.

Visuals play a critical role too. Striking images of wildfires, melting glaciers, and floods are used to paint a stark picture. While these issues are indeed serious, the constant barrage of these extreme scenarios can lead to what psychologists call 'crisis fatigue' – where you become desensitised to the crisis itself.

Moreover, the projection of extreme scenarios often comes with a ticking clock. Phrases like "we have only 12 years left to act" create a sense of urgency. This technique, known as time-bound pressure, aims to compel immediate action by suggesting that delay could result in missed chances to prevent disaster.

The psychology behind fear-based environmental messaging

Understanding the psychology behind these fear-based tactics is key to recognising why they are so effective. The fundamental principle at play is the human brain's hard-wiring to prioritise immediate threats. This is an evolutionary trait; our ancestors had to react quickly to threats like predators to survive. Today, when you hear that your environment is under immediate threat, it triggers a similar 'fight or flight' response.

Fear also has a unique ability to unite people. When faced with a common enemy, in this case climate change, communities might feel a stronger bond amongst each other. However, this can lead to an 'us vs. them' mindset, where people who are sceptical of climate change narratives are seen as outsiders or adversaries, further polarising discussions.

Another psychological aspect is the narrative of control or the lack thereof. Fear-based messages often make you feel that the situation is out of your control unless drastic actions are taken. This can lead to anxiety and a feeling of helplessness, which isn't conducive to constructive or rational decision-making.

Comparing climate fear-mongering to other historical examples

To put climate fear-mongering into perspective, let's compare it to other historical examples. During the Cold War, the threat of nuclear war was a constant source of fear. Governments used propaganda to prepare citizens for a potential atomic attack, instilling a culture of fear. This had various societal impacts, including the building of bomb shelters and the stigmatization of dissenting voices who were often labelled as sympathisers of the enemy.

In the 1970s, the global cooling scare is another instance where media propagated a coming ice age. Magazines and newspapers speculated on massive food shortages and catastrophic drops in temperatures. Much like today, these stories were based on some scientific observations, but were blown out of proportion for sensational effect.

Similarly, the Y2K bug created a fear that the turn of the millennium would bring about technological chaos. As the year 2000 approached, stories of planes falling from the sky and nuclear plants melting down were rampant. Billions were spent in preparing for a disaster that ultimately was much less severe than publicised.

These historical examples show how fear has been used as a tool to influence public opinion and policy. While the threats were real to varying degrees, the way they were presented often exaggerated the immediate danger, overshadowing rational debate and measured responses.

In each of these cases, and in the current climate narrative, fear can overshadow other important aspects of the conversation. It can stifle meaningful debate, encourage polarisation, and lead to decisions driven more by panic than by thoughtful consideration of facts. As you navigate through the myriad of information about climate change, it's crucial to approach what you hear and see with a critical mind. Recognise the difference between genuine concern and manipulation, and seek out sources and solutions that aim for a balanced, constructive discussion about our planet's future.

Navigating the narratives around climate change requires a keen eye and a resilient mind. By understanding the techniques used to spread fear, the psychological impacts of such strategies, and their historical usage, you are better equipped to sift through sensationalism and contribute positively to the environmental discourse. Remember, change is necessary, but how we approach that change determines the quality and effectiveness of our response.

RECAP AND ACTION ITEMS

As you've navigated through the complexities of the climate agenda, it's clear that this isn't just about science; it's deeply intertwined with politics, social perceptions, and even manipulation through fear. Understanding these layers is crucial because it helps you see beyond the surface narratives to the often-unseen motives and influences at play.

Firstly, recognising how political agendas shape climate policies is vital. Policies aren't always crafted purely on scientific evidence but are frequently influenced by political gain or pressure from various interest groups. As a proactive citizen, you can make a difference by staying informed about the policy-making processes and the role of lobbying. Engage with and support policies that are transparent and scientifically sound. Consider reaching out to your local representatives to express your views on the importance of unbiased, science-based climate legislation.

Secondly, the phenomenon of virtue signalling can dilute genuine environmental efforts. While it might seem benign, this practice can create a facade of concern rather than fostering real change. You can counter this by critically evaluating environmental claims and initiatives. Support organisations and initiatives that provide clear, tangible results and avoid those that seem to prioritise image over action. Promoting awareness about the difference between mere symbolism and actionable environmental efforts is also a powerful step you can take.

Lastly, the use of fear-mongering to influence public opinion on climate issues can lead to paralysis rather than action. Understand the psychological impact of fear-based messaging and strive to engage with sources that offer solutions and inspire hope rather than despair. Sharing balanced, factual information about climate change with your community can help combat the fear-driven narrative.

In conclusion, your role in this vast ecosystem of information and influence is not just as a passive observer but as an active participant. By critically analysing the information you come across, supporting transparent and effective policies and initiatives, and fostering informed discussions within your circles, you contribute to a more rational and effective environmental movement. Remember, every small step counts in the journey towards a more sustainable and truthful approach to addressing climate change.

2

THE GREENING EFFECT OF CO2

"To cherish what remains of the Earth and to foster its renewal is our only legitimate hope of survival." - **Wendell Berry**

Photosynthesis Boost

Imagine a world where every breath you take is not only sustaining you but also fuelling a vast, unseen network of growth and rejuvenation. That's right, we're talking about the magic of photosynthesis, a process that's quietly been given a boost courtesy of rising CO2 levels. Let's take a closer look at how this increased carbon dioxide in our atmosphere could be enhancing plant growth, bolstering agricultural yields, and even aiding forest recovery and expansion.

Increased Plant Growth

It's basic science: plants absorb carbon dioxide during photosynthesis to produce energy and growth. So, it stands to reason that higher levels of CO_2 could supercharge this natural process. Recent studies suggest that this isn't just a theory; it's happening right now. Across the globe, from the dense Amazonian rainforests to the vast Siberian taiga, satellite data have shown a trend of "greening" over large parts of Earth's vegetated areas.

But what does this mean for you and me? Well, for starters, more CO_2 means plants require less water to perform photosynthesis. This increased water-use efficiency can be particularly beneficial in arid regions where water is scarce. Plants becoming larger and more robust also means they are better able to withstand the stresses of varying climatic conditions. This resilience could be crucial as weather patterns become more unpredictable with climate change.

However, it's not all a bed of roses. This boost in growth isn't uniform across all species or ecosystems, which might lead to ecological imbalances. Faster-growing plants could outcompete slower ones, potentially altering natural habitats and the wildlife that depends on them. So, while the initial picture looks rosy for plant growth, the ecological tapestry is complex.

Enhanced Agricultural Yields

On the agricultural front, rising CO_2 levels could be a game-changer. With the global population projected to reach 9.7 billion by 2050, food production needs to ramp up by about 70%. More CO_2 could be part of the solution. Experiments with crops like wheat, rice, and soybeans have shown that increased carbon dioxide can enhance growth rates and yields. This phenomenon, known as CO_2 fertilisation, could significantly boost food security and play a pivotal role in feeding the growing global population.

For farmers, this could mean more robust crops that not only grow faster but are possibly more resistant to pests and diseases. The implications here are vast. Enhanced yields could stabilise food prices, which often fluctuate due to crop failures and shortages. However, it's important to temper optimism with caution. The benefits of CO_2 fertilisation may be limited by factors such as nutrient availability — more CO_2 doesn't automatically mean more nutrients in the soil.

Moreover, while some regions might see a boom in agricultural productivity, others might not experience any benefit at all. This disparity could widen existing economic gaps between agricultural communities, particularly in less developed countries where access to technology and modern farming techniques is limited.

Forest Recovery and Expansion

Forests are the lungs of our planet, absorbing CO_2 and giving back oxygen. The role of increased CO_2 in aiding forest recovery and expansion is a fascinating area of study. In many parts of the world, deforestation has led to significant environmental and ecological damage, including loss of habitat, biodiversity, and climatic instability. However, with higher levels of CO_2, there's potential for quicker and more robust forest regeneration.

Studies have shown that young forests in particular can absorb a substantial amount of CO_2, which accelerates their growth and helps in their expansion. This rapid growth not only helps in carbon sequestration but could also aid in restoring ecosystems faster than previously thought possible. The implications for wildlife, and for communities that rely on forests for their livelihood, could be profound.

Yet, this isn't a one-size-fits-all solution. The type of species, soil quality, and local climate conditions all play crucial roles in how effectively forests can utilise this extra CO_2. Additionally, increased forest biomass must be managed responsibly to prevent subsequent issues like increased fire risk due to denser forests.

In wrapping up this exploration into the photosynthesis boost provided by CO_2, it's clear that while there are several potential benefits, there are also significant complexities and considerations. The greening effect of CO_2 could indeed be playing a pivotal role in shaping a more resilient and abundant planet, but this is just one piece of the vast puzzle of global ecology. As we continue to delve deeper into understanding these dynamics, the insights gained will be crucial in guiding sustainable practices and policies that not only benefit us but also future generations.

Revisiting Climate Models

CO2's Role in the Models

When you delve into the labyrinth of climate modelling, the role of CO2 often takes centre stage. These models, complex mathematical representations used to predict future climate conditions, heavily rely on assumptions about carbon dioxide and its effect on global warming. But here's something that might tickle your curiosity: CO2 isn't just a villain in the climate narrative; it also wears a hero's cape in some respects.

To understand how, let's break it down a bit. Carbon dioxide is a greenhouse gas, which means it traps heat in the atmosphere. Without it and its greenhouse gas buddies, Earth would be as cold and lifeless as a forgotten rock floating in space. However, the concentration of CO2 is crucial. While too much of it leads to excessive warming, it's also indispensable for photosynthesis—the process through which plants convert sunlight into energy, with CO2 being one of the raw materials.

Climate models attempt to simulate the balance of CO2's effects. They predict how changes in its concentration influence global temperatures, weather patterns, ocean currents, and more. But it's crucial to remember that these models are based on current scientific understanding, which evolves with every new study. They are not crystal balls but educated guesses equipped with statistical probabilities.

Historical Climate Data vs. Predictions

Comparing historical climate data with model predictions is akin to comparing a meticulously kept diary with a series of expert opinions about future events based on that diary. Climate models use historical data to calibrate their predictions, adjusting parameters until the model output aligns with what has been observed in the past. This retrospective fitting is both a strength and a limitation.

For instance, if you look at climate models from 20 or 30 years ago, you'll notice that many significantly underestimated the rate of Arctic Sea ice decline. Why? Because they couldn't account for all the variables influencing ice melt, some of which were poorly understood at the time. On the flip side, some aspects of climate change, like the increase in extreme weather events, have been more accurately predicted.

This discrepancy between historical data and predictions highlights the inherent uncertainty in climate modelling. Models are continually refined as new data comes in and as our understanding of Earth's climate system improves. It's a dynamic, ongoing process—more of a marathon than a sprint. This means that while models are useful for planning and preparation, they should be seen as guides rather than prophets.

Modelling Accuracy

The accuracy of climate models is a hot topic—no pun intended. It's crucial to acknowledge that while these models are sophisticated tools that have improved significantly over the decades, they are not infallible. Each model comprises numerous assumptions and estimates which can affect its output.

One of the main challenges in climate modelling is the complexity of Earth's climate system. It's an intricate interplay of atmospheric conditions, land surfaces, ice sheets, and oceans. Each component interacts with the others in complex ways that are difficult to predict. For instance, clouds can both cool the Earth by reflecting sunlight back into space and warm it by trapping heat. The net effect of clouds is still one of the most challenging aspects of climate modelling.

Moreover, there's the issue of scale. Global models provide a big-picture view but often miss finer details. Regional climate models fill in some gaps by offering more detailed predictions for specific areas. However, these too have limitations, particularly when it comes to predicting the impacts of climate change on local ecosystems or weather phenomena like hurricanes and droughts.

Despite these challenges, it's important to recognise the value of climate models. They are crucial in helping scientists, policymakers, and the public understand potential future scenarios and make informed decisions. By continuously updating and refining these models with the latest scientific data and improved computational techniques, their accuracy and reliability will only increase.

As you can see, the role of CO_2 in climate models, the comparison with historical data, and the ongoing improvements in modelling accuracy are all pivotal in shaping our understanding of climate change. While far from perfect, these models provide a crucial framework for anticipating and mitigating the effects of increased CO_2 levels. As we move forward, embracing both the limitations and strengths of climate modelling will be key to navigating the complexities of climate change effectively.

Environmental and Economic Benefits

When you start peeling back the layers on the impacts of CO_2, it's not just the climate and the biosphere where you find significant changes; there are tangible shifts in both the economic and environmental sectors too. Let's dive into how an increase in CO_2 could potentially reshape our economic landscape while offering some environmental benefits.

Lower Energy Costs

You might wonder how on Earth CO_2 could play a role in lowering energy costs. It's a fair query. The link isn't straightforward, but it's there. Higher levels of CO_2 have been shown to enhance plant growth and agricultural productivity, which in turn influences bioenergy sources. Bioenergy crops are plants specially grown for conversion into energy. Faster-growing plant species, which flourish in enriched CO_2 environments, can produce more biomass. This biomass can then be converted more efficiently into biofuels or burnt in biomass power plants to generate electricity.

Moreover, enhanced CO_2 levels could potentially reduce the need for artificial plant growth stimulants in agriculture and forestry, which frequently involve energy-intensive production processes. By naturally boosting plant growth, CO_2 could indirectly lead to a reduction in the energy consumed and the costs associated with these processes.

Another angle is the impact of CO_2 on renewable energy sources like solar and wind. While these technologies themselves don't directly interact with CO_2 levels, the economic environment influenced by CO_2 could accelerate the adoption of renewables. As governments and corporations push towards carbon neutrality, investments in renewable energy could see a boost, leading to advancements in technology, increased efficiency, and ultimately, lower costs for consumers.

Reduced Dependency on Imports

In a world where countries are increasingly conscious of their carbon footprints, managing CO_2 emissions has become a geopolitical lever. Countries rich in fossil fuels have traditionally held significant power due to the dependency of others on their exports. However, with the global shift towards sustainability, this power dynamic could shift.

If you're living in a country that imports a substantial amount of its energy needs, this shift could be particularly relevant. Enhanced CO2 levels benefiting local agriculture and energy sectors could reduce dependence on external sources. This doesn't just have economic implications; it also enhances national security by making countries less vulnerable to foreign energy supply shocks and geopolitical tensions.

Think about it: if a country can produce more of its own food and generate more of its own energy, the need to entangle itself in complex, and sometimes unstable, international relationships diminishes. This could lead to a more stable economic environment with potentially lower prices for you, the consumer, and less volatility in response to international events.

Increased Food Production

This is where the rubber meets the road in terms of direct benefits to you and communities worldwide. Enhanced CO2 levels can lead to what is known as 'CO2 fertilisation', which we've touched on briefly. This process can significantly boost the productivity of farms by enhancing photosynthesis, the method by which plants convert sunlight into energy.

In a world with ever-increasing mouths to feed, the potential for increased food production cannot be overstated. By increasing the yield of crops per hectare, CO2 could help in producing more food from the same amount of land. This not only helps in feeding a growing global population but could also stabilise food prices. Volatility in food prices often leads to economic instability, which can have ripple effects throughout economies—particularly in less developed countries where a large portion of income is spent on food.

Furthermore, increased agricultural yields could free up land for other uses, including reforestation or natural habitats, which in turn contributes to biodiversity and further captures CO_2—a virtuous cycle of sorts. This isn't just good news for farmers and agricultural conglomerates; it's potentially transformative for everyday people around the world.

In wrapping this up, it's clear that the narrative around CO_2 isn't as black and white as it may seem. While it's vital to approach this topic with caution and a robust understanding of the broader implications of rising CO_2 levels, the potential environmental and economic benefits, particularly in terms of lower energy costs, reduced dependency on imports, and increased food production, offer a compelling angle that deserves your attention. As we continue to seek truth and understanding in the climate dialogue, these facets provide crucial context that can help in shaping informed, effective policies and personal decisions in the face of global warming.

RECAP AND ACTION ITEMS

So, you've journeyed through the intriguing realm of CO_2's greening effect. You've explored how increased CO_2 levels can boost plant growth, enhance agricultural yields, and potentially aid in forest recovery and expansion. You've delved into the complexity of climate models, comparing historical climate data with predictions to scrutinize CO2's role and the accuracy of these models. And, you've considered the environmental and economic benefits, such as lower energy costs, reduced dependency on imports, and increased food production.

Now, armed with this knowledge, what next? It's time to translate insights into action. Here are a few steps you can take:

1. Educate Others: Start conversations. Whether it's over dinner or during a meeting, share what you've learned about the nuanced roles of CO2. Education is the foundation of change.

2. Support Sustainable Practices: Choose to support businesses and initiatives that prioritize sustainable practices in agriculture and energy. Your consumer choices have the power to change market trends.

3. Engage with Policymakers: Voice your thoughts to local representatives. Advocate for policies that recognise both the challenges and potential benefits of rising CO2 levels within the context of broader environmental management.

4. Stay Informed: The science of climate change is constantly evolving. Keep up-to-date with the latest research and discussions. A well-informed public is more resilient and proactive.

5. Invest in Green Technology: Consider investing in green technologies either directly or by choosing financial instruments that support eco-friendly businesses. This not only aids in reducing dependency on imports but also bolsters the growth of sustainable energy sources.

By understanding the dual-edged nature of CO_2 — its benefits and its broader implications on climate — you are better equipped to engage in informed debates and make choices that contribute positively towards our planet's future. Remember, every small step can lead to significant changes. So, take these actions, spread the word, and be part of a global solution to a global challenge.

3

THE REALITIES OF RENEWABLE ENERGY

"We cannot command Nature except by obeying her." – Francis Bacon

Understanding Renewable Limitations

In the vibrant dialogue about climate change and the shift towards sustainable energy, renewable resources like solar and wind power often appear as the knights in shining armour. However, while they play a crucial role in our battle against global warming, these technologies come with their own set of challenges that can't be ignored. Let's peel back the layers and explore some of these limitations.

The Intermittency Issue of Solar and Wind Power

First up, let's chat about intermittency. It's a fancy word that essentially means solar and wind power can be as unpredictable as a British summer. The sun doesn't always shine, and the wind doesn't always blow, which creates a significant reliability issue for these energy sources. This isn't just an inconvenience; it's a major hurdle for energy providers who need to ensure a constant power supply.

For example, on a sunny day, solar panels might produce an abundance of energy, more than you could use. But come nighttime, their output plummets to zero. Similarly, wind turbines thrive on blustery days but stand eerily still when the air is calm. This variability means that relying solely on these sources can lead to power shortages or the need for excess energy production at peak times.

Energy providers, therefore, must have backup systems in place, typically from more stable, but less green, sources like natural gas. This necessity dilutes the environmental benefits of renewable resources and complicates the logistics of integrating them into the national grid.

The Challenge of Energy Storage

Addressing the intermittency issue leads us directly to our next point: energy storage. If only we could bottle up that midday sunshine or the gusty winds at midnight for later use! Well, storing energy is indeed possible, but it's neither simple nor cheap.

Current technologies for storing renewable energy primarily involve batteries, and while advancements have been made, these are not without their drawbacks. Lithium-ion batteries, for example, are the most popular choice for solar energy storage. They're the same batteries you use in your smartphones and laptops but on a much larger scale. Although effective, they are expensive and have a limited lifespan, which requires frequent replacements and has a considerable environmental footprint.

Furthermore, the capacity of these batteries isn't yet at a level where they can store enough power for large populations or for prolonged periods of no renewable energy production. This limitation highlights a significant gap in our quest to rely entirely on renewable sources.

Geographic and Climatic Limitations of Renewables

Finally, let's turn our attention to the geographic and climatic limitations of renewable energy sources. Not every location is suited for every type of renewable energy. Solar panels, for instance, are less effective in areas with low sunlight, such as countries far from the equator or regions that experience long winters.

Wind turbines also have their specific requirements. They need to be placed in locations with consistent and strong winds, which are not available everywhere. Plus, the installation of wind farms can be controversial, as they require a lot of space and can impact local wildlife and scenery.

These geographic and climatic factors mean that the potential for renewable energy varies dramatically from one place to another. It's not a one-size-fits-all solution, and this variability must be considered when planning national energy strategies. Countries need to assess their own natural resources carefully and might find that a hybrid approach, combining several different types of renewable energies, along with traditional sources, is necessary.

As we navigate through these limitations, it becomes clear that while renewable energy is an essential part of our move towards a more sustainable future, it's not a magic bullet. The transition to renewables needs to be managed with a keen understanding of their intermittency, storage challenges, and geographical dependencies. But don't let these hurdles dishearten you. Each challenge also presents an opportunity for innovation, driving us towards more sophisticated and efficient solutions as we continue our journey towards sustainable energy.

The Economics of Renewables

Cost Analysis of Renewable vs Traditional Energy

When you stack up the numbers, the financial landscape of energy is like a tale of two cities. On one front, we have the traditional stalwarts—oil, coal, and natural gas—fuels that powered our great-grandparents' lives and still largely support our modern world. On the other, there are the bright-eyed newcomers: solar, wind, hydro, and their renewable cousins, who've been making waves in energy markets worldwide.

Historically, renewable energy sources have been criticised for their high initial costs compared to their fossil-fuelled counterparts. This critique, however, is increasingly part of a bygone era. The price of producing one megawatt-hour from solar photovoltaics (PV) dropped by about 89% between 2009 and 2019, according to figures from Bloomberg NEF. Wind power saw a similar price plunge, with costs decreasing by around 70% in the same period.

Yet, it's not just about how much cheaper renewables have become; it's about understanding the full economic implications of each energy source. When considering renewables, you must factor in the 'levelised cost of energy' (LCOE). This metric helps compare different methods of electricity production on a consistent basis by considering the total lifecycle costs divided by energy output.

Another crucial economic consideration is the operational and maintenance costs. Fossil fuels often require expensive exploration, extraction, transportation, and refining. Renewables typically have lower operational costs once they are up and running—think no fuel costs and reduced maintenance expenses due to fewer moving parts.

Despite these promising figures, it's vital to acknowledge that direct cost comparisons can oversimplify the broader economic implications. External costs, such as environmental damage and health impacts related to fossil fuel usage, aren't always factored into the sticker price of coal and oil but have real economic consequences.

Subsidies and Financial Support for Renewables

Navigating through the world of energy economics without bumping into subsidies would be like trying to find your way through London without a map—possible, but not recommended. Subsidies have played a crucial role in the renewable sector, acting as both accelerators and protectors.

In many regions, governments have implemented subsidy schemes like feed-in tariffs (FiTs), tax incentives, and grants to encourage the adoption of renewable technologies. These financial incentives are designed to make renewable projects more economically attractive and feasible by offsetting initial costs and providing long-term financial security.

For example, the UK's Contracts for Difference (CfD) scheme protects renewable electricity generators from volatile wholesale prices by paying them the difference between the market price and a fixed 'strike price'. This sort of subsidy provides a predictable revenue stream, making it easier for projects to secure financing. in the US there is no similar scheme at the federal level, although there are State level schemes like Renewable Portfolio Standards (RPS) / Clean Energy Standards (CES) and Feed-in Tariffs (FiTs) which provide the same basic protection.

Critics often argue that such subsidies artificially deflate the cost of renewables, making them appear more viable than they might be under pure market conditions. However, it's essential to remember that fossil fuels have historically received substantial subsidies as well. A 2021 study by the International Monetary Fund estimated global fossil fuel subsidies at $5.9 trillion in 2020, which includes direct subsidies and the failure to charge for pollution and other externalities.

The current trend is towards reducing these subsidies as renewable technologies become more cost-competitive. This shift is crucial for creating a level playing field in the energy market and ensuring that renewables can stand on their own economic merits.

Long-Term Economic Impacts of Renewable Investments

Investing in renewable energy isn't just a spending decision—it's an investment in the future. The long-term economic impacts of shifting towards renewables can be profound, influencing everything from global markets to local job creation.

One of the most compelling arguments for renewable investments is the potential for economic diversification. By reducing dependency on imported fuels, countries can improve their energy security and balance of trade. Additionally, the renewable sector can drive job creation in new industries ranging from technology manufacturing to system installation and maintenance.

Moreover, renewables can contribute to more stable energy prices in the long term. Fossil fuel markets are notoriously volatile, subject to geopolitical tensions and fluctuating supply dynamics. Renewable energy sources, particularly wind and solar, have no fuel costs and minimal operational costs, leading to more predictable pricing.

The transition to a low-carbon economy also opens up significant opportunities in green finance. Green bonds and other sustainable investment vehicles are growing, allowing investors to support environmental projects while potentially earning returns. This trend not only helps direct capital towards sustainable projects but also signals a broader economic shift towards valuing long-term, sustainable growth over short-term gains.

As you delve deeper into the economics of renewable energy, it becomes clear that the narrative is not just about costs and subsidies; it's about investing in a sustainable infrastructure that supports economic stability and growth while safeguarding the environment. The journey towards a fully renewable energy system might be fraught with financial, technical, and regulatory challenges, but the economic potential is as vast as it is vital for our future.

Technological Advances and Setbacks

Recent Technological Innovations in Renewable Energy

In the ever-evolving landscape of renewable energy, technological innovations continue to push the boundaries of what's possible, transforming how you consume energy. Solar and wind power technologies have seen significant advancements, enhancing their efficiency and integration into the energy grid.

One of the standout innovations in solar technology has been the development of perovskite solar cells. These cells are not only cheaper to produce than traditional silicon-based cells but also offer higher efficiency and flexibility. This means they can be used in more diverse applications, from windows that generate electricity to coatings on vehicles. Such versatility could potentially broaden solar energy's appeal and accessibility.

Wind energy isn't lagging behind either. The introduction of larger, more aerodynamic turbine designs has enabled substantial increases in power output. These turbines use lightweight materials and innovative blade designs that optimise wind capture at lower wind speeds. Moreover, floating wind turbines have unlocked the potential for offshore installation in deeper waters where winds are stronger and more consistent, significantly boosting energy generation.

Another groundbreaking area is the integration of Artificial Intelligence (AI) and machine learning into renewable energy systems. AI algorithms help predict energy demand and supply fluctuations more accurately, improving energy grid management. They can also optimize the operation of wind turbines and solar panels, adjusting angles and outputs in real-time based on weather conditions to maximise efficiency.

Limitations in Current Renewable Technology

Despite these technological leaps, several limitations persist, which can sometimes slow the pace at which renewables are adopted. One of the primary issues is the energy density of renewable sources. Solar and wind energy, while abundant and sustainable, do not yet match the energy density provided by fossil fuels, which means they require much larger physical spaces to generate equivalent amounts of energy. This can be a significant barrier in densely populated or geographically limited areas.

Another challenge is the durability of renewable energy technologies. For instance, solar panels and wind turbines are exposed to environmental wear and tear, which can affect their lifespan and efficiency. The degradation of solar panel performance over time due to exposure to the elements is an ongoing concern. Similarly, wind turbines need to withstand varied and harsh weather conditions, making robust engineering a necessity but also driving up costs.

The intermittency of power supply—a topic you're already familiar with—is another technological hurdle. The sun doesn't always shine, and the wind doesn't always blow, making energy storage solutions critical. However, current battery technologies, while improving, still struggle to store energy at the scale needed for large grid applications both efficiently and cost-effectively.

The Potential Future of Energy Technology

Looking ahead, the future of renewable energy technology holds promising solutions to these current limitations, potentially revolutionizing how you interact with energy.

Energy storage technology is one area poised for significant breakthroughs. Innovations like solid-state batteries promise higher energy densities and faster charging times while being safer and more environmentally friendly than lithium-ion counterparts. There is also ongoing research into using hydrogen as a storage medium, which could be a game-changer for managing surplus renewable energy efficiently.

In solar technology, the development of organic photovoltaic cells presents an exciting frontier. These cells, made from carbon-based materials, offer a lightweight, flexible alternative to traditional solar panels. They can be printed using roll-to-roll processes, drastically reducing manufacturing costs and enabling new applications such as integrating photovoltaics into building materials or even clothing.

On the wind energy front, advances in materials science might lead to even more durable and efficient turbine designs. Scientists are experimenting with bio-inspired designs, such as those mimicking the natural properties of spider silk, to develop blades that are both stronger and more resilient.

Moreover, the integration of renewable systems with smart grid technologies could lead to more robust energy networks that manage supply and demand more efficiently. Smart grids use digital communication technology to react to changes in energy usage and supply dynamically, facilitating a smoother integration of renewable sources.

As you navigate the complexities of the renewable energy landscape, these technological advancements and potential future innovations offer a glimpse into a more sustainable and efficient future. While there are setbacks and challenges, the path forward is illuminated by continuous innovation and the relentless pursuit of better and more adaptable renewable energy solutions.

RECAP AND ACTION ITEMS

As we've delved deep into the nitty-gritty of renewable energy, it's clear that while it's not a silver bullet, it remains a critical component of our fight against climate change. We've seen how solar and wind power face limitations like intermittency and geographical constraints, and how the journey towards efficient energy storage is still very much a work in progress. Despite these hurdles, the economic argument for renewables is becoming increasingly convincing, not least because of dropping costs and the long-term financial benefits.

However, the transition to renewable energy is not just a matter for policymakers and industry giants; it involves you too. Here are some practical steps you can take to make a meaningful impact:

1. Stay Informed: Knowledge is power. Continue to educate yourself about the latest developments in renewable technology and energy policies. This will not only allow you to make informed decisions but also enable you to engage in meaningful discussions and advocate effectively.

2. Reduce Energy Consumption: Start with the basics. Lowering your energy usage is a no-brainer when it comes to reducing your carbon footprint. Consider energy-efficient appliances, reduce waste, and be mindful of your consumption habits.

3. Support Green Energy: Where possible, switch to a green energy provider or consider investing in renewable energy solutions for your home, such as solar panels. Yes, there's an upfront cost, but the long-term savings and environmental impact are worth considering.

4. Vote with Your Wallet: Support businesses and products that are committed to sustainable practices and renewable energy. Consumer demand can drive significant change, influencing companies to adopt greener solutions.

5. Engage Locally: Get involved in local environmental groups or initiatives that promote renewable energy projects. Whether it's advocating for policy changes or participating in community solar projects, local action can lead to big results.

6. Speak Out: Use your voice to advocate for renewable energy solutions and policies. Contact your representatives, participate in discussions, and use platforms, both online and offline, to push for change.

By integrating these actions into your daily life, you not only contribute to the global shift towards renewables but also set a precedent for responsible and sustainable living. Remember, every small step counts in our collective journey towards a greener future.

4

THE DARK SIDE OF RENEWABLES

"Technology is a useful servant but a dangerous master." - Christian Lous Lange

Land Use and Biodiversity

In the dialogue about climate change, renewable energy usually takes the spotlight as the hero of our story. Solar panels gleam in the sun, and wind turbines stand tall like modern-day windmills fighting against carbon giants. But, as in every good story, complexities lurk beneath the surface. The quest for a sustainable future might have some unintended consequences, particularly when it comes to land use and biodiversity. Let's delve deeper into this side of the narrative that's not often told.

Deforestation for Solar Farms

Imagine walking through a dense forest, the air fresh with the scent of pine and earth. Now picture that same forest, but replace the trees with rows upon rows of solar panels. It's a stark image, isn't it? Solar farms require significant land areas to be effective. In the pursuit of green energy, vast tracts of land are being transformed, and quite ironically, not always for the better.

Forests are not just groups of trees; they are ecosystems supporting diverse forms of life. When these wooded areas are cleared to make way for solar farms, the immediate loss is twofold: the trees that absorb CO_2 are gone, and the habitat for countless species disappears. This isn't just about losing a couple of squirrels. We're talking about potentially disrupting whole populations of flora and fauna that depend on this habitat. In regions where land is scarce, the choice of location for solar farms becomes critically important. Placing them on deforested land rather than natural, untouched areas could be a start, but the question remains: are we replacing one evil with another?

Wind Turbines and Wildlife Disruption

Wind energy is hailed as one of the cleanest energy sources. However, the towering turbines that are synonymous with wind energy are not without their faults. The spinning blades of wind turbines pose a significant threat to flying wildlife, particularly birds and bats. These creatures use the wind currents that turbines inhabit, leading to fatal encounters.

The problem extends beyond just the mortality rates of these animals. There's a disruption in migration patterns and a decrease in population in areas surrounding wind farms. It's a ripple effect: when you affect one species, you inadvertently impact the entire ecosystem. Birds, for instance, play crucial roles in ecosystems such as pest control, plant pollination, and seed dispersal. The disruption or decrease of bird populations in certain areas can lead to unforeseen consequences on local flora and other fauna.

Moreover, the noise and vibration produced by wind turbines have shown to affect terrestrial wildlife, altering breeding patterns and reducing habitat usability. The footprint of a turbine might seem small on the ground, but its impact on the surrounding environment can be vast.

Habitat Loss

Beyond specific examples with solar farms and wind turbines, the broader issue of habitat loss looms large. Renewable energy installations often take up a considerable amount of space. This space often overlaps with natural habitats. In our race to scale up renewable energy infrastructure, are we considering the spaces we consume?

For instance, large hydroelectric dams, while providing substantial renewable energy, often lead to significant ecological and environmental changes, including altering river ecosystems and affecting the aquatic life that depends on them. Similarly, the push for bioenergy crops leads to large-scale changes in land use, often replacing natural vegetation that numerous species depend on with monocultures.

The challenge here is finding a balance. Energy needs are increasing, and renewable energy provides a promising solution to the looming crisis of climate change. However, the implementation of these technologies must be done thoughtfully. Strategic planning that considers not just the immediate human needs but also long-term ecological sustainability is crucial. This might include placing solar panels on rooftops and brownfields instead of forests, or designing wind farms that are less disruptive to wildlife.

As we navigate these complex decisions, your awareness and engagement are more crucial than ever. Understanding the full spectrum of impacts associated with renewable energy can lead to more informed decisions and discussions. After all, the goal is not just to replace fossil fuels with renewables but to create a truly sustainable future that harmoniously includes both human and ecological needs.

Resource Drain and Pollution

When we talk about the shiny, hopeful prospects of renewable energy, it's easy to picture a clean, green future. Solar panels glistening in the sunlight, wind turbines majestically turning in the breeze—it all seems so pristine. But behind these idyllic images lies a less talked about reality: the significant resource drain and pollution that can accompany renewable energy production. Let's peel back the layers and look at what's really going on.

Mining for Rare Earth Metals

First up, let's dive into the world of rare earth metals. These are not your everyday metals; they have unique properties that make them essential for the powerful magnets needed in wind turbines and advanced batteries used in solar energy systems. Sounds cool, right? But here's the rub: extracting these metals is anything but clean.

Mining for rare earth metals is a heavy-duty process that often involves stripping large areas of land. The extraction process typically uses a cocktail of toxic chemicals, which can leach into the soil and waterways, posing a risk to ecosystems and human health. For instance, in areas like Baotou in Inner Mongolia, the quest for these metals has created what many refer to as an environmental disaster zone, with waters so polluted that they can no longer support aquatic life.

Moreover, the irony is stark—technologies designed to help us cut down on pollution are, in this instance, a source of it. While efforts are being made to improve the sustainability of these mining operations, they are currently far from being environmentally benign.

Waste from Solar Panels

Transitioning to solar energy, the image of waste might not immediately come to mind. Yet, the lifecycle of a solar panel is not entirely devoid of environmental impact, especially at the end of its life. Solar panels are complex devices containing metals like lead and cadmium, which can be hazardous if the panels are broken or disposed of improperly.

Currently, the recycling processes for solar panels are not keeping pace with the amount being installed. This gap leads to significant amounts of waste, which often end up in landfills, potentially releasing toxic materials into the environment. As the use of solar panels increases, so does the urgency to find efficient, cost-effective ways to recycle them. The challenge is immense, and while solutions like improved recycling technologies are on the horizon, they're not yet at scale.

Lifecycle Emissions of Renewables

Finally, let's talk about lifecycle emissions. It's a term that gets thrown around a lot, but what does it really mean? Essentially, it refers to the total emissions of greenhouse gases that occur during the lifecycle of a renewable energy source, from production to disposal. Yes, renewables generally emit far fewer greenhouse gases than fossil fuels when they are in use, but their production, installation, and decommissioning can still contribute significantly to their total environmental footprint.

Take wind turbines, for example. The production of these

towering giants involves large amounts of steel and concrete—materials that require a lot of energy to produce and transport. Although wind energy does not produce emissions while generating electricity, the construction and setup stages can be quite carbon-intensive. Moreover, decommissioning old turbines is not only costly but also poses significant environmental challenges.

The same goes for solar panels and bioenergy plants; each has its own set of lifecycle emissions that, if not managed properly, could undermine the very benefits they offer in terms of reducing atmospheric CO_2. Recognising and addressing these emissions is crucial for truly maximising the environmental benefits of renewable energy technologies.

As you can see, the path towards a renewable future is not as straightforward as it might initially appear. The transition to renewable energy is essential for combating climate change, no doubt about it. However, understanding and mitigating the environmental costs associated with resource drain and pollution is equally imperative. As we continue to innovate and improve these technologies, let's keep our eyes open to the full picture—balancing the scales between our green aspirations and the grey realities they sometimes entail.

Economic Impact

Cost of Renewable Energy Subsidies

Let's dive straight into the murky waters of renewable energy subsidies. You might have heard that these subsidies are the lifeline of the renewable sector, essential for their survival and growth. True, but there's more to this story. Subsidies are essentially financial support provided by governments to make renewable energy sources more competitive against their fossil-fuelled counterparts. Sounds straightforward, right? But here's the rub: these subsidies need to come from somewhere, which means taxpayer money.

Now, the question you might be asking is: "How much are we talking about here?" Globally, renewable energy subsidies have seen a significant uptick, scaling to billions annually. The exact figures can vary wildly from one country to another, based on policy, the maturity of the renewable energy market, and political will. For instance, in the UK, the total public expenditure on renewable energy subsidies has been substantial, aiming to achieve a greener grid.

But what does this mean for you? Well, while supporting green energy is noble and necessary for battling climate change, these subsidies can also distort the energy market. They might lead to an overreliance on government money, potentially stifling innovation in newer and more efficient technologies. Additionally, if not carefully structured, subsidies can oversupply the market, leading to problems like negative pricing where too much power floods the grid at times, actually leading to prices that dip below zero.

Impact on Electricity Prices

Moving on, let's talk about how this ties into electricity prices – something that directly hits your wallet. Integrating renewable energy into the national grid isn't just a plug-and-play scenario. It requires an overhaul of existing infrastructure, which is neither easy nor cheap. These costs, again, often wind up on your bill.

Renewables, especially solar and wind, are intermittent energy sources – the sun doesn't always shine, and the wind doesn't always blow. This intermittency means that the grid needs backup power sources, like gas or hydro, ready to jump in, which adds to the complexity and cost. Moreover, the initial investment for creating renewable-friendly grids is high. This setup needs to be recouped, and guess where that cost often ends up? Yes, on your electricity bill.

There's also the cost of upgrading transmission lines to handle the decentralised input of renewables. Traditional power plants are usually located near urban centres and have robust infrastructure to transmit electricity. Renewable sites, like wind farms and solar panels, are often in remote areas, requiring new networks that can handle fluctuating energy levels.

Job Losses in Traditional Energy Sectors

Finally, let's consider the human angle – jobs. The shift towards renewables isn't just a technological shift but a significant economic one too. As renewable energy becomes more dominant, traditional energy sectors, notably coal and oil, are seeing a downturn. This transition, though beneficial for the planet, has real-world consequences for those employed in these sectors.

Regions historically reliant on industries like coal mining have faced economic downturns, leading to significant job losses. For instance, the decline of coal mines due to a shift towards cleaner energy sources has been stark. While renewable sectors are indeed job creators, the types of jobs they provide, and where they are located, often do not compensate for the losses in traditional sectors. The skill set required can be different, and geographic dislocation can occur, meaning the people losing jobs aren't necessarily the ones gaining new ones.

Moreover, the job creation rate in renewables, while positive, doesn't always match the number of jobs lost in other sectors. The mismatch can lead to economic and social disruptions in communities that once depended on traditional energy sectors.

Navigating the economic impacts of renewable energy isn't just about appreciating the benefits but understanding the complexities and real costs involved. While the transition to a greener future is necessary, it's also essential to manage it in a way that balances economic impacts, ensuring a just transition for all involved. As you reflect on these points, consider not only the environmental but also the economic landscapes that will shape the future of energy.

RECAP AND ACTION ITEMS

As we've explored the complexities surrounding renewable energy, it's clear that while they offer solutions to some of our most pressing environmental issues, they also come with their own set of challenges. From the significant land use and biodiversity impacts to the resource drain and pollution, and finally, the economic implications, it's evident that the path to a sustainable future isn't straightforward.

However, knowledge is power. Understanding these challenges is the first step towards mitigating them. Here are practical steps you can take to contribute to a more informed and balanced approach to the adoption of renewable energy:

1. Stay Informed: Continue educating yourself about the environmental impacts of renewable technologies. Knowledge will empower you to make better decisions and advocate effectively.

2. Support Responsible Practices: Encourage policies and companies that adopt sustainable practices in the production and deployment of renewable technologies. Look for certifications and standards that ensure minimal environmental impact.

3. Promote Biodiversity: Engage with and support local and national initiatives that aim to preserve and restore natural habitats. This could range from reforestation projects to wildlife conservation programs that are designed to coexist with renewable energy projects.

4. Advocate for Recycling Programs: With the increase in waste from solar panels and other renewable technologies, pushing for robust recycling programs will help mitigate the environmental impact. You can do this by supporting legislation or companies that prioritise end-of-life processing for these technologies.

5. Participate in Community Energy Planning: Get involved in your community's energy planning to advocate for a balanced approach that considers both the benefits and impacts of renewables. Community involvement can influence local policies and decisions.

6. Reduce Personal Energy Use: Lastly, while engaging on a larger scale, don't underestimate the power of personal action. Reducing your energy consumption and increasing your energy efficiency are immediate steps you can take to lessen the burden on our planet.

By taking these steps, you not only contribute to a more sustainable approach to renewable energy but also help pave the way for a future where economic growth and environmental sustainability are not at odds. Let's work together to refine, improve, and innovate our way towards truly sustainable energy solutions.

5

THE DEPENDENCE ON CONVENTIONAL ENERGY

"The Stone Age didn't end for lack of stone, and the oil age will end long before the world runs out of oil." – Sheikh Ahmed Zaki Yamani, former Saudi Arabian Minister of Oil

The Role of Fossil Fuels

In the modern world, fossil fuels are like that old pair of jeans you can't seem to throw away. They're familiar, reliable, and even when you know it's time for a change, parting ways seems daunting. Let's delve into why this dependence persists, the unique advantages these energy sources offer, and how geopolitics plays a significant role in the global energy landscape.

Why Global Economies Still Rely on Fossil Fuels

You might wonder why, with all the buzz around solar and wind power, we're still clinging to coal, oil, and natural gas. It boils down to a few critical factors: infrastructure, cost, and energy density.

Firstly, the infrastructure for extracting, refining, and distributing fossil fuels is profoundly entrenched. This network has been developed over decades and represents a massive investment by numerous economies. Transitioning away from this established system isn't just about switching fuel sources; it's about overhauling or replacing a colossal global apparatus.

Cost is another persuasive factor. Despite advances in renewable technologies, fossil fuels often remain the cheaper option for generating electricity, especially in developing countries where cost constraints are tighter. The immediate affordability of fossil fuels continues to make them an attractive option for many.

Lastly, energy density—the amount of energy stored in a given system or space—is significantly higher in fossil fuels than in current renewable alternatives. This makes them especially useful in applications where high energy output is required in a compact form, such as in aviation and many industrial processes.

The Benefits of Fossil Fuels That Renewables Currently Can't Match

While it's clear that renewables like wind and solar are crucial for a sustainable future, there are areas where fossil fuels still hold the upper hand. Availability and reliability are at the forefront. Fossil fuels can provide power 24/7, regardless of weather conditions or time of day. In contrast, solar and wind power are intermittent, depending on the weather and daily cycles, thus requiring storage solutions or backup systems to ensure a constant energy supply.

Another benefit is energy storage and transport. Oil, for instance, can be easily transported around the world in tankers and stored for long periods, providing energy security for countries that rely on imports to meet their energy needs. Developing similar flexibility for renewables requires significant advancements in battery and other storage technologies, which are currently in progress but not yet at a global scale.

Moreover, many industries rely on the high temperatures generated by burning fossil fuels for processes like cement and steel production. Developing renewable alternatives that can meet these industrial requirements poses a significant challenge and is an area where fossil fuels continue to be indispensable.

The Geopolitics of Oil and Gas

The geopolitics of fossil fuels is a dramatic tale of power, influence, and, occasionally, conflict. Countries that possess substantial fossil fuel reserves often have considerable leverage on the global stage. Think about nations like Saudi Arabia, Russia, and the United States. These countries wield significant influence not just because of their military or economic power, but because they supply the world with its lifeblood—energy.

Control over oil and gas reserves can lead to wealth and power for nations, but it also makes them targets for geopolitical strategies and conflicts. The desire to control energy sources and supply routes has been a central theme in numerous international conflicts and continues to shape foreign policies worldwide.

Additionally, this dynamic creates a dependency that can discourage nations from transitioning to renewable energy sources. For importers of oil and gas, the volatility in prices and the potential for supply disruptions can have severe economic impacts. Yet, the fear of losing a stable supply often keeps them locked in a fossil fuel embrace.

Fossil fuels have painted a complex and intricate picture in the tapestry of global energy consumption. Understanding this picture—acknowledging the challenges in moving away from fossil fuels, appreciating the benefits they still offer, and recognising the geopolitical chessboard they create—is crucial. It's not just about advocating for change but understanding what that change entails for a deeply interconnected world. As we move forward, the journey from fossil fuels to a sustainable energy future appears both necessary and fraught with challenges. But understanding these complexities is the first step in navigating our way through them.

Nuclear Energy: A Misunderstood Alternative?

The Basics of Nuclear Power

Let's dive straight into the mechanics of nuclear energy, shall we? It's a powerhouse of a topic, but understanding it is less about complex physics and more about seeing its potential in plain sight. Nuclear power plants operate on the principle of nuclear fission. This is where atoms, typically of uranium, are split into smaller parts in a controlled environment. When these atoms split, they release a significant amount of heat. This heat is then used to boil water, producing steam, which spins turbines to generate electricity. Simple, right?

Despite its somewhat intimidating reputation, the process is similar to how a conventional power plant works, except the heat is derived from nuclear reactions rather than burning fossil fuels. This fundamental difference is what makes nuclear energy a low-carbon alternative. Yes, you heard right—low-carbon. The nuclear reactions themselves do not produce carbon dioxide as a byproduct, which is a significant win for the environment.

Debunking Common Myths About Nuclear Energy

Now, onto some myth-busting. Nuclear energy suffers from a severe PR problem, and it's time to clear the air. One of the most pervasive myths is that nuclear energy is unsafe. The images of Chernobyl and Fukushima loom large in public memory, but these are exceptions rather than the rule. Modern nuclear technology has evolved leaps and bounds in terms of safety protocols and design. Reactors now come equipped with multiple, foolproof safety systems that are designed to prevent the type of accidents that are etched in our collective memories.

Another myth is that nuclear waste is an unsolvable problem. It's true, nuclear waste is a challenge, but it's not an insurmountable one. Technological advancements have led to more efficient ways of recycling and reprocessing spent fuel, reducing its volume and toxicity. Plus, the actual volume of nuclear waste is much smaller compared to the waste produced by fossil fuels when you consider the lifecycle emissions and pollutants.

Lastly, there's this idea that nuclear energy is bad for the environment. Let's get some perspective—the primary environmental concern with nuclear energy is the thermal pollution and potential for harmful impacts if waste management is mishandled. However, compared to the continuous and extensive damage from extracting and burning fossil fuels—think oil spills, destruction of habitats for mining, air and water pollution—the environmental footprint of nuclear power is significantly smaller.

Comparing Safety Records of Nuclear and Other Energies

When you stack nuclear energy against other forms of energy in terms of safety records, things look surprisingly positive. Let's lay down some facts. Statistically, nuclear power is one of the safest forms of energy in terms of deaths per kWh produced. Yes, accidents have occurred, and their impacts have been grave, but these are incredibly rare events. On the other hand, deaths related to the extraction and transportation of fossil fuels, as well as pollution-related health issues, occur on a daily basis and on a much wider scale.

Coal, oil, and natural gas plants all emit particulate matter, sulphur dioxide, and nitrogen oxides, which have direct and well-documented health risks including respiratory problems, heart disease, and cancer. The World Health Organization attributes millions of deaths worldwide to air pollution predominantly from fossil fuels.

In contrast, the nuclear industry is subject to stringent safety checks and constant international scrutiny. The design of modern reactors incorporates multiple safety systems that function on the principle of redundancy and fail-safety: if one system fails, another steps in immediately to prevent accidents. Moreover, the industry learns from each incident. Post-Fukushima, safety protocols were revamped globally, enhancing the already tight measures in place.

While it's crucial to acknowledge and learn from past nuclear incidents, it's equally important to recognise the advancements in technology and safety that significantly minimise any risks.

The transition from older-generation reactors to newer, safer designs continues to enhance the safety credentials of nuclear power.

In essence, nuclear energy stands as a misunderstood giant in the energy landscape. It holds the potential to support massive reductions in carbon emissions while providing stable and reliable power. Debunking the myths and understanding the robust safety records compared to other energy sources is crucial in any informed debate about our energy future. As we look towards a cleaner, more sustainable energy configuration, nuclear energy's role appears not just beneficial, but necessary.

Bridging the Gap

Transition strategies from fossil fuels to renewables, hybrid systems and their benefits, future predictions for energy consumption.

The journey from fossil fuels to renewables isn't just a simple hop, skip, and a jump. Rather, it's akin to building a bridge while walking on it — complex but crucial. As we navigate this transition, the strategies we use need to be both innovative and practical, ensuring that while we aim for a sustainable future, we also meet the present energy demands.

Transition Strategies from Fossil Fuels to Renewables

You've probably heard the buzzwords: "clean energy," "sustainable future," and perhaps even "net-zero emissions." But how do we actually get from our current heavy reliance on fossil fuels to a future dominated by renewables? The answer lies in a meticulously crafted blend of policy, technology, and consumer behaviour.

One of the first steps is the decarbonisation of the power sector. This move involves ramping up investments in renewable energy sources like solar, wind, and hydropower. For instance, solar panels and wind turbines are already becoming fixtures in landscapes around the world. However, integration of these technologies into the existing grid is not without challenges. The variability of renewable energy sources means that they don't produce electricity as consistently as fossil fuels. This is where energy storage systems come in, such as batteries, which can store excess energy generated during peak conditions for use during low-production periods.

Another significant strategy is the implementation of carbon pricing. By putting a price on carbon emissions, it nudges businesses to cut down on their carbon footprint and invest in cleaner technologies. While this might sound like a straightforward solution, its implementation can be fraught with political and economic challenges. The key is to set a price that reflects the true environmental cost of carbon emissions without placing undue burdens on consumers, particularly in lower-income brackets.

Energy efficiency also plays a pivotal role. This isn't just about making more energy-efficient devices; it's about rethinking how energy is used in industries, homes, and transportation. For instance, retrofitting old buildings with better insulation and energy-efficient appliances can significantly reduce energy demand.

Hybrid Systems and Their Benefits

As we pivot to renewables, hybrid energy systems can serve as an effective bridge. These systems combine various forms of energy generation, like wind and solar, with more consistent sources of power, such as natural gas or nuclear energy, to create a more reliable energy supply.

One of the greatest benefits of hybrid systems is their ability to mitigate the intermittency issues associated with renewable energy. For example, on cloudy or non-windy days when solar panels and wind turbines might underperform, natural gas turbines can quickly ramp up to fill the gap, ensuring a steady energy supply.

Moreover, hybrid systems can be tailored to regional needs. In regions abundant in sunlight, solar can be the dominant player in the mix, backed up by bioenergy or hydroelectric power during less sunny periods. Similarly, coastal areas might leverage a combination of offshore wind and marine energy. This flexibility not only optimises the use of local resources but also enhances energy security by reducing reliance on imported fuels.

Future Predictions for Energy Consumption

Looking ahead, the global energy landscape is expected to undergo significant transformations. The International Energy Agency (IEA), for instance, predicts that renewable energy will meet 80% of the growth in global electricity demand by 2030. This shift is anticipated as countries intensify their efforts to combat climate change and as renewable technologies continue to advance and become more cost-effective.

Electric vehicles (EVs) are set to play a crucial role in reducing the consumption of fossil fuels. With advancements in battery technology and an increase in charging infrastructure, EVs are becoming a more viable option for consumers around the world. This not only cuts down on oil consumption but also significantly reduces urban air pollution.

In terms of industrial energy consumption, there's growing interest in hydrogen as a clean fuel option. Hydrogen can be produced from renewable energy sources and holds potential for heavy industries like steel and chemical manufacturing, which are challenging to decarbonise using electricity alone.

As these trends suggest, the future of energy consumption will likely be characterised by a diverse mix of sources. The transition will require not only technological innovation but also a commitment from governments, businesses, and individuals to rethink and reshape the way energy is produced, consumed, and conserved.

In navigating this transition, it's crucial to remain adaptable and open to exploring various energy solutions. This isn't just about switching off one source and turning on another; it's about reimagining our entire energy ecosystem to create a sustainable and resilient future. As you witness these changes unfold, remember that every small step in reducing carbon emissions and enhancing energy efficiency contributes to a larger global impact.

RECAP AND ACTION ITEMS

We've unpacked the hefty suitcase of conventional energy, starting with the enduring reliance on fossil fuels. You now understand the tough-to-match benefits they provide and the complex geopolitics that keep the oil and gas sectors spinning. Then, we ventured into the realm of nuclear power, demystifying its operation and debunking the myths that often cloud its perception. Safety comparisons highlighted that, when managed correctly, nuclear could be a remarkably safe energy source.

Now, let's talk about what you can do moving forward. Transitioning from fossil fuels to renewable energies is not just a necessity but an inevitability. The journey involves embracing hybrid systems that combine the reliability of conventional energy with the sustainability of renewables. These systems are stepping stones, critical in the shift towards a greener planet.

Here are some practical steps you can take:

1. Educate Yourself and Others: Knowledge is power. The deeper your understanding, the better you can advocate for changes in energy policies and practices. Share what you've learned about the complexities of energy sources with others. Discussions can lead to revelations and eventually, action.

2. Support Clean Energy Initiatives: Whether it's by voting for policies that promote renewable energies, investing in clean energy companies, or even choosing a green energy plan for your home, every little action contributes to a larger change.

3. Reduce Energy Consumption: Start with your personal habits. Simple changes like improving home insulation or using energy-efficient appliances can lessen your reliance on conventional energy sources.

4. Stay Informed About Technological Advances: The energy sector is rapidly evolving. By keeping up-to-date with the latest technologies in both renewables and hybrids, you can make informed decisions about what you support and where you invest your money.

5. Advocate for Balanced Policy Making: Engage with local and national policymakers. Advocacy for balanced policies that support a gradual transition to renewable resources is crucial. Policies need to support innovation in the energy sector while ensuring economic stability and energy security.

The shift from conventional to renewable energy isn't just a technical transition; it's a cultural shift. By taking these steps, you can contribute to a sustainable future, ensuring that the planet remains hospitable and vibrant for generations to come. Remember, every bit counts when we're talking about the health of our planet. Let's make those bits positive and proactive.

6

THE TRUE COST OF RISING FUEL PRICES

"When you tug at a single thing in nature, you find it attached to the rest of the world."
– John Muir

Poverty and Inequality

When fuel prices skyrocket, the ripple effects reach far beyond just the petrol or gas stations. It's an intricate web that entangles the most vulnerable sections of society, exacerbating poverty and widening the chasm of inequality. Let's unpack this, shall we?

Energy Affordability

Imagine this: you're budgeting to the last penny, and then the cost of heating your home, cooking your meals, or even getting to work suddenly spikes. This isn't just a hypothetical for millions around the world; it's their daily grind. As fuel prices climb, the cost of energy becomes less affordable for everyone, but it hits those with lower incomes the hardest.

Energy is not a luxury; it's a fundamental need, akin to water and food. Yet, when prices rise, it becomes a significant part of monthly expenses, forcing some uncomfortable choices. Should you heat your home or cut back on food expenses? These decisions are real and wrenching for many families.

The issue extends to electricity bills too. In many regions, electricity is generated using fossil fuels, so the cost of electricity is directly tied to fuel prices. For families already on the brink, this could mean the difference between having the lights on and sitting in the dark.

Impact on Lower-Income Families

For families with limited financial flexibility, rising fuel costs can mean reallocating funds from essential areas such as health care, education, or nutritious food to cover the increased energy expenses. This reallocation can have long-term consequences on the health and well-being of these families. Children might miss out on educational opportunities, or health issues might be neglected, setting a cycle of hardship that can persist across generations.

Moreover, consider the psychological impact. The stress of managing these financial tightropes can lead to increased anxiety and depression among parents, which in turn affects the whole family dynamics. It's a heavy burden to carry, knowing that your financial situation is not just a personal issue but one that casts a shadow over your entire family's future.

Global Inequality

Now, let's zoom out and look at this from a global perspective. Developing countries, where a large chunk of the population might already be struggling, face an even steeper uphill battle when fuel prices surge. These nations often lack the infrastructure to support wide-scale deployment of alternative energy sources, making them heavily dependent on traditional fuels.

This dependency traps these countries in a vicious cycle: economic development stalls as energy costs rise, and investments in clean energy or other infrastructure are deferred in favour of immediate, albeit costly, solutions. It's not just about individual families anymore; it's about entire nations grappling with slowed progress and deepening poverty.

Moreover, the international playing field becomes uneven. Wealthier nations can cushion their citizens against the shocks of rising fuel prices through subsidies or by tapping into strategic reserves. Meanwhile, poorer countries might see their already scant resources stretched thinner, exacerbating global inequality.

As you can see, the spike in fuel prices isn't just a matter of changing numbers at the petrol or gas station. It's a complex issue that feeds into broader socio-economic challenges. The struggle for energy affordability, the disproportionate impact on lower-income families, and the exacerbated global inequalities form a narrative that is as compelling as it is critical.

Addressing these issues requires nuanced, informed debates and innovative solutions — something we'll explore further in our journey through the unseen green. So, keep this context in mind as we delve deeper into the intricacies of climate myths, debates, and solutions. Your understanding of these foundational issues is crucial as we navigate the broader discussions of climate change and sustainability.

Food Security Challenges

When you think about rising fuel prices, you might first consider the impact on your travel costs, heating bills, or the price at the pumps. However, one of the most critical areas influenced by these spikes is often less immediately visible until you hit the supermarket aisles. Yes, we're talking about food security. The journey from farm to fork relies heavily on fuel, and as prices climb, the ripples affect everyone, especially the most vulnerable populations around the globe.

Increased Cost of Food Production

The first hurdle comes at the very beginning of our food supply chain: production. Modern agriculture is heavily mechanised, from the tractors ploughing fields to the combine harvesters and the vehicles that transport produce to processing plants and stores. A jump in fuel prices means it costs more to run all these machines. For instance, diesel is a lifeline on the farm, and its price directly affects the cost of operating machinery.

The increase doesn't stop at machinery operations. Many agricultural inputs like fertilisers and pesticides are petroleum-based products. Hence, as crude oil prices soar, so do the costs of these essential items. The result? It becomes pricier to grow food. This isn't just about individual farmers seeing their expenses spike; it's about entire production costs escalating, which then trickles down through the supply chain to you, the consumer.

But there's more. Irrigation, another critical component of food production in many arid regions, also depends significantly on fuel-powered pumps. With increased fuel costs, maintaining optimal irrigation becomes more expensive, potentially reducing crop yields if farmers attempt to cut costs by watering less.

Effects on Agriculture

This increase in production cost leads us seamlessly into the broader effects on agriculture. Farmers, especially those operating on thin margins in competitive markets, face tough choices. Do they absorb the costs, reduce the quality or quantity of their output, or pass the cost increases onto wholesalers and eventually, to you?

In developed countries, larger agricultural enterprises might weather these increases through efficiencies or subsidies, but small to medium-sized farms feel the pinch profoundly. These farms are often less able to invest in energy-efficient technologies that could mitigate some costs, leaving them more vulnerable to fuel price volatility.

For developing countries, the scenario is even more daunting. Many farmers in these regions are subsistence farmers who grow just enough food to feed their families and perhaps sell a small amount for income. For them, increased costs can mean the difference between getting by and not having enough to eat. They might be forced to revert to even less efficient, labour-intensive methods that don't require fuel but result in lower yields.

Moreover, agriculture in less developed areas often lacks the infrastructure that could alleviate some of these challenges. Poorer road networks mean that transporting goods to market already consumes more fuel, and price hikes can make these costs prohibitive, leading to food wastage and loss of income for farmers, exacerbating the cycle of poverty and food insecurity.

Risk of Starvation

Now, let's touch on the gravest consequence of all this: the risk of starvation. As dramatic as it sounds, the reality is that for many around the world, rising fuel prices could push them over the edge into food insecurity, which can lead to starvation and severe malnutrition.

Price increases in food production and transportation costs mean that at every stage, costs are being added. These costs accumulate and lead to higher prices at the grocery store. For families already struggling to make ends meet, this can mean having to make tough choices about what and how much to eat.

Countries that rely heavily on food imports are particularly vulnerable. These nations will have to deal with both the internal challenges of higher fuel prices and the added costs imposed by exporting countries passing on their increased production costs. For countries dealing with economic instability, currency devaluation can exacerbate the situation, making imports prohibitively expensive.

Moreover, in crisis-hit regions, where humanitarian aid is crucial, higher fuel prices can hamper the efforts of relief organisations. The cost of delivering essential supplies, including food, increases, potentially reducing the volume of aid that can be delivered or increasing its cost to untenable levels.

In essence, the domino effect of rising fuel prices stretches far beyond just paying more at the pump. It permeates through the entire agricultural sector and hits hardest at those who are already vulnerable. As fuel prices rise, so does the risk that more people around the world will go hungry.

This chain of events places an undeniable strain on global food security—an issue that requires not only immediate attention but sustainable, long-term strategies to ensure that a spike in fuel prices doesn't lead to a spike in hunger.

Alternative Solutions

When tackling the multi-headed hydra of rising fuel prices, the instinct might be to throw up our hands and declare it an unbeatable foe. But, as with many of life's complex problems, a cocktail of creative solutions can offer a way forward. Let's dive into some of the most effective strategies that not only counteract the sting of fuel price hikes but also pave the way for a more sustainable and equitable future.

Energy Diversification

One of the first steps towards mitigating the impact of rising fuel costs is diversification. You've likely heard the saying, "Don't put all your eggs in one basket." This wisdom holds true for energy sources as well. By broadening the energy mix, countries can shield themselves from the volatility of global oil markets which often leave consumers at the mercy of unpredictable price spikes.

Renewable energy sources like wind, solar, and hydroelectric power offer the most promise. These technologies have seen dramatic improvements in both efficiency and cost-effectiveness over the last decade. For instance, the cost of solar panels has plummeted, making solar installations more accessible to a broader segment of the population. Moreover, these energy sources are immune to the geopolitical tensions that frequently affect fossil fuel prices.

In countries like the UK, where wind power now accounts for a significant portion of the energy mix, consumers have seen not only stabilisation in energy costs but also a decrease in carbon emissions. Diversification doesn't just provide an economic buffer – it aligns closely with the urgent need to reduce our carbon footprint.

Subsidies and Support for Vulnerable Populations

While transitioning to renewable energy is a vital long-term strategy, it's also crucial to address the immediate needs of those most affected by rising fuel costs. Lower-income families often spend a larger proportion of their income on energy, making them particularly vulnerable to price increases. Here, targeted subsidies and financial support can play a pivotal role.

Consider the approach of subsidised energy tariffs for low-income households, or direct financial assistance to help cover energy bills. These measures can provide a lifeline for those in dire straits. However, it's important that these subsidies are carefully designed to encourage energy-saving behaviours rather than perpetuate high consumption patterns.

Another innovative approach could be the introduction of energy banks, akin to food banks, which provide energy credits to those in need. These could be funded through a combination of government support and contributions from energy providers.

Investing in Energy Efficiency

Finally, let's talk about getting more bang for your buck – or more precisely, more warmth for your watt. Investing in energy efficiency is arguably one of the most cost-effective measures to combat the impact of rising fuel prices. Simple changes in household and industrial energy use can lead to significant savings and reductions in demand.

For households, this might mean upgrading to energy-efficient appliances, improving insulation, or installing smart thermostats that optimise heating and cooling. Governments can incentivise these upgrades through grants and tax rebates. The beauty of this approach is that it not only reduces the energy bill but also decreases the overall energy consumption, which in turn, lessens the environmental impact.

On a larger scale, industries can adopt more efficient processes and technologies. For example, the use of heat recovery systems and high-efficiency boilers can dramatically reduce energy use in manufacturing. Moreover, the adoption of modern agricultural techniques can minimise the fuel consumed in food production and transport, addressing the issues of food security discussed earlier.

Energy efficiency also extends to the urban planning level. Creating compact, walkable cities with robust public transport networks can significantly reduce the need for personal vehicles, which are major fuel consumers. Such urban designs not only promote a healthier lifestyle but also foster a sense of community.

Each of these strategies – from diversifying our energy sources to enhancing energy efficiency – represents a piece of the puzzle in addressing the challenges posed by rising fuel prices. While no single solution is a magic bullet, together they form a robust defence, turning a formidable challenge into manageable segments. As you reflect on these strategies, consider how each might be implemented in your community or influence your personal energy choices. After all, change starts with informed, proactive decisions.

RECAP AND ACTION ITEMS

By now, you've navigated through the intricate layers of how rising fuel prices impact poverty and inequality, challenge our global food security, and what alternative solutions might look like. It's clear that the issue stretches far beyond mere numbers on a price tag—it seeps into every crevice of societal stability and personal well-being.

Firstly, consider the pressing issue of energy affordability. As you've seen, this isn't just about keeping the lights on; it's about ensuring that every individual has access to the basic services that enable a dignified life. What can you do? Start by advocating for policy changes that support energy subsidies for lower-income families. Engage with local community projects that aim to improve energy efficiency in homes, which can significantly reduce living costs for the most vulnerable.

Next, the ripple effects on food security cannot be ignored. The increase in production costs directly affects the price of food, putting a strain on everyone, especially those in already precarious financial situations. Here, you might focus on supporting local agriculture. Buying locally not only reduces the carbon footprint associated with long-distance food transportation but also supports your local economy. Additionally, consider donating to or volunteering with organisations that work to combat food insecurity. Every small action contributes to a larger impact.

Lastly, the path forward must include a diversified energy approach. Moving away from a reliance on fossil fuels requires innovation, investment, and public support. You can play a role by staying informed and supporting renewable energy initiatives. Whether it's by installing solar panels, participating in community energy projects, or simply advocating for clean energy policies, your involvement is crucial.

Remember, while the problems are complex, the steps you take don't have to be monumental. Small, consistent actions can drive significant change. It's about making informed choices, advocating for equitable policies, and supporting the communities most affected by these global issues. Each step you take not only helps mitigate the impact of rising fuel prices but also contributes to a more sustainable and just world.

7

THE UNSUNG HERO: NATURAL GAS

"Natural gas is the bridge fuel that can power our economy with less of the carbon pollution that causes climate change." - Barack Obama

Natural Gas and Agriculture

When you think about natural gas, your mind might first jump to heating homes or fuelling power stations. But there's a lesser-known yet crucial role it plays directly in the fields of our farms. Yes, agriculture—a cornerstone of human civilization, heavily reliant on the power of natural gas. Let's dig a bit deeper, shall we?

Fertiliser Production from Methane

The journey begins with methane, a primary component of natural gas. It's a potent greenhouse gas, yes, but also an invaluable resource in the production of ammonia, which is used to create nitrogen fertilisers. The process, known as the Haber-Bosch process, synthesises ammonia by combining nitrogen from the air with hydrogen, which is derived from methane in natural gas through a method called steam reforming.

Why does this matter to you? Well, without nitrogen fertiliser, produced through this process, global food production would likely plummet. It's estimated that around half of the food grown globally today relies on synthetic nitrogen fertilisers. Without them, the yield of most of our staple crops would be significantly reduced, impacting food availability and prices globally.

The efficiency of the Haber-Bosch process has improved dramatically since its inception, leading to a decrease in the amount of natural gas required per unit of fertiliser produced. However, it still consumes a considerable amount of natural gas—about 3-5% of the world's natural gas supply goes into fertiliser production. This shows just how intertwined our food supply and natural gas really are.

Boosting Global Food Supply

Moving on from the creation of fertilisers, natural gas steps up again in its role in boosting the global food supply. As the global population continues to grow, with projections suggesting a reach of nearly 9.7 billion by 2050, the pressure on food production is immense. Here, natural gas provides a solution, not just in fertiliser production but also in powering various agricultural operations, including irrigation systems and food processing facilities.

In addition, natural gas is used in greenhouse operations to manage temperatures and to generate carbon dioxide to promote plant growth. This application is particularly pivotal in regions with harsh climates, where outdoor farming is not feasible year-round. By leveraging natural gas in such controlled environments, food production becomes less seasonal, more predictable, and highly efficient.

Yet, while the role of natural gas in enhancing food security is clear, it brings us to an inevitable question about its sustainability. Can this resource be part of a long-term solution given the environmental challenges we face?

Sustainability of Natural Gas

This brings us to a critical juncture. The sustainability of natural gas in agriculture, like in other sectors, is often debated. On one hand, natural gas burns cleaner than coal and oil, emitting about 50 to 60 percent less carbon dioxide when combusted in a new, efficient natural gas power plant compared with emissions from a typical new coal plant. This aspect, coupled with its efficiency in production and various applications, makes it appear as a more sustainable option.

However, the environmental footprint of natural gas extends beyond its combustion. The extraction and transportation of natural gas can result in methane leaks—another potent greenhouse gas. Addressing these leaks is crucial in reducing the overall environmental impact of natural gas usage.

Moreover, the concept of sustainability encompasses not just environmental dimensions, but economic and social ones as well. From an economic perspective, natural gas has generally been favourable due to its relatively low and stable price, making agricultural operations more predictable and less vulnerable to energy price swings. Socially, the role of natural gas in bolstering global food security and enabling farming in otherwise inhospitable regions can be seen as positive.

Nevertheless, as renewable energy technologies advance and become more economically viable, the role of natural gas could see a shift. The transition towards greener alternatives could affect how natural gas is perceived in the spectrum of sustainability. This transition is not immediate but is a consideration that needs attention if we are to balance our immediate needs with long-term sustainability goals.

In wrapping up this part, it's clear that natural gas plays a multifaceted role in agriculture—from producing the very fertilisers that feed our crops to powering the energy-intensive processes involved in modern farming. Its impact on food security in a burgeoning global population is undeniable. Yet, the dialogue about its sustainability is not black and white but requires a nuanced understanding of both its benefits and its broader environmental implications. As with many resources we rely on today, the key lies in managing its use wisely and conscientiously, ensuring it serves our needs today without compromising our world tomorrow.

Economic Advantages

When diving into the economic perks of natural gas, it's like unearthing a buried treasure in your own backyard. Not only does it keep the home fires burning quite literally, but it also stabilises our energy bills and plays a pivotal role in the ongoing energy debate. Let's break this down into digestible chunks, shall we?

Lowering Heating Costs

First off, let's chat about how natural gas can reduce heating costs. In the chilly embrace of winter, when the frost paints your windowpanes, heating isn't just a comfort; it's a necessity. Now, you might be wondering how natural gas steps into this frosty picture. It comes down to efficiency and cost-effectiveness. Natural gas heaters, for instance, are incredibly efficient. They can convert up to 90% of their fuel into heat. Compared to electric heaters, which might have efficiency ratings hovering around 30%, it's clear that natural gas isn't just blowing hot air.

Moreover, the cost factor plays a huge role. Natural gas is generally cheaper than electricity, which is often generated from more expensive (and sometimes less environmentally friendly) resources like coal or oil. This cost difference can be significant, depending on where you live. For the average household, switching from electric heating to natural gas can save substantial amounts on utility bills. So, it's not just about staying warm; it's about keeping your wallet from freezing over too.

Stability of Natural Gas Supply

Moving onto the stability of natural gas supply. Now, here's where things get interesting. Unlike oil, which often travels a tumultuous path from distant and sometimes politically unstable regions, a large proportion of natural gas is sourced closer to home. For instance, many countries have substantial natural gas reserves, making them less dependent on the geopolitical whims that can disrupt oil supplies.

This stability is crucial not just for keeping the lights on but also for planning our future energy needs. Utilities can invest in natural gas infrastructure knowing that the resource will be there long-term, allowing for better budgeting and less financial volatility. This kind of predictability is a cornerstone of economic stability, which in turn can foster broader economic growth. Businesses and industries that rely heavily on energy can plan their budgets with greater certainty, knowing that their energy supply isn't going to vanish or spike in price overnight.

Natural Gas vs. Renewables

Finally, let's tackle the elephant in the room: natural gas versus renewables. This is a hot topic, with opinions flaring on both sides. But let's sift through the noise and focus on the facts. Renewable energy sources like solar and wind are pivotal in our march towards a sustainable future. Yet, they come with their own set of challenges, primarily around intermittency – the sun doesn't always shine, and the wind doesn't always blow.

This is where natural gas swings in like a reliable friend. It's an excellent partner for renewable energy because it's flexible and can quickly ramp up production when solar panels and wind turbines take a break. This partnership allows a stable flow of energy to be maintained, ensuring that energy supply remains constant and reliable, even when renewables aren't able to shoulder the load.

Moreover, in terms of infrastructure and technology, transitioning directly from coal or oil to renewables isn't a walk in the park. It requires building new systems and technologies, which can be costly and time-consuming. Natural gas acts as a bridge, offering a cleaner alternative to coal and oil while the renewable infrastructure catches up.

So, while it's clear that the future is steering towards renewables, natural gas is not just a stopgap. It's a critical enabler, making the transition smoother and less disruptive economically.

In wrapping up this exploration into the economic advantages of natural gas, it's evident that this resource isn't just another cog in the energy machine. From keeping your home cosy without breaking the bank to stabilising our energy supplies and smoothing the path towards renewable energy, natural gas plays several vital roles in our ongoing energy narrative. As we continue to debate and shape our energy future, understanding these facets helps you see why natural gas is often hailed as an unsung hero in the complex world of energy economics.

Environmental Considerations

When you peel back the layers on natural gas, its environmental impact is a mixed bag. This energy source, often hailed as a cleaner alternative to coal, does come with its set of challenges. Let's dive into what this means for our planet, particularly focusing on methane leaks and management, natural gas' emissions compared to coal, and its role in transitioning to a low-carbon future.

Methane Leaks and Management

Methane, the primary component of natural gas, is a potent greenhouse gas. It traps heat in the atmosphere far more effectively than carbon dioxide, at least in the short term. This makes the management of methane leaks a crucial environmental issue.

The natural gas supply chain—from extraction to transportation to distribution—is plagued with opportunities for methane to escape into the atmosphere. These leaks are more than just a safety hazard; they have significant implications for climate change. According to various studies, methane is about 84 to 87 times more potent than CO_2 over a 20-year period. This means that even small leaks can have a substantial impact on global warming.

The good news? The technology to reduce these emissions is already available. Enhanced leak detection and repair practices (LDAR) can significantly cut down on unintentional releases. Innovations such as infrared cameras and portable analysers are making it easier and cheaper to detect leaks quickly and accurately.

However, the implementation of these technologies is inconsistent. Regulation plays a big role here. In regions with stringent environmental regulations, companies are more likely to invest in methane management. In contrast, in areas where such regulations are lax or non-existent, methane emissions tend to be higher.

Comparisons with Coal Emissions

Natural gas burns cleaner than coal; that's a fact. When you burn natural gas, it produces about half as much carbon dioxide, less than a third as much nitrogen oxides, and one percent as much sulphur oxides as coal combustion. This has positioned natural gas as a 'bridge fuel', an energy source that can help transition the global economy from high to low carbon emissions.

However, this comparison isn't without its caveats. The aforementioned methane leaks can, to some extent, negate the benefits of lower carbon dioxide emissions. If the rate of methane emissions from natural gas systems is greater than about 3%, the climate benefits of switching from coal to natural gas are lost.

Moreover, while natural gas emits less particulate matter than coal, it's not zero. The extraction and burning of natural gas still release pollutants that can affect air quality and public health. It's a cleaner option, yes, but not entirely clean.

Role in Transition to Low-Carbon Future

The role of natural gas in the transition to a low-carbon future is perhaps one of the most hotly debated topics in energy circles. On one hand, it's seen as a necessary step away from more polluting fuels like coal and oil. On the other, some argue that investing in natural gas infrastructure and technology diverts attention and resources from renewable energy sources like wind and solar.

One of the key advantages of natural gas is its ability to complement renewable energy sources. Natural gas power plants can quickly be ramped up and down, making them ideal for balancing the grid when intermittent renewables like solar and wind are not available. This flexibility helps maintain a stable and reliable energy supply, which is crucial as we increase our reliance on renewables.

However, the risk is that natural gas could become too entrenched, delaying the transition to truly clean energy sources. The infrastructure for natural gas is expensive, and once built, there's a financial incentive to keep using it as long as possible. This could potentially lock in certain emissions for decades.

Moreover, the development of 'green' technologies like biogas and renewable natural gas (RNG) is also changing the landscape. These technologies promise to produce gas with a net-zero carbon footprint, although they are currently at a nascent stage and not yet at a scale to meet global demand.

In conclusion, natural gas does have a role to play in our current energy landscape, but it's not without its environmental challenges. Methane management, a clear understanding of its emissions profile compared to coal, and strategic use in complementing renewable energy are crucial factors. As we move forward, the focus should be on minimising the environmental impact while maximising the benefits as part of a broader, sustainable energy strategy. It's a delicate balance, but one that needs careful navigation as you, the informed reader, continue to explore the complexities of our global energy choices.

RECAP AND ACTION ITEMS

As we've navigated through the multifaceted role of natural gas in our society, it's clear that while it presents certain advantages, it also carries significant environmental responsibilities. Let's distil what we've covered into actionable insights that you can use to make informed decisions and initiate discussions about our energy future.

Firstly, the role of natural gas in agriculture, specifically in fertiliser production, is undeniable. It has helped boost global food supply significantly. However, it's vital to continuously assess and improve the sustainability of these processes. You can contribute by supporting and advocating for research into more efficient and less environmentally damaging fertiliser production methods.

Economically, natural gas offers some benefits like lower heating costs and a stable supply which can be particularly attractive when compared to the intermittency issues faced by some renewables. Yet, this doesn't mean it should be a permanent solution. Engage with local and national energy policies to encourage a balanced approach that also accelerates the integration of renewable energy sources, ensuring that natural gas acts as a bridge in the transition to a fully renewable energy system.

Environmental considerations bring us to the crux of the matter. Methane leaks are a serious concern that mitigates some of the emissions advantages natural gas has over coal. It's crucial to support technologies and policies that aim to drastically reduce these leaks. Moreover, understanding that natural gas is cleaner than coal but still a fossil fuel is essential. Advocate for and participate in initiatives that promote cleaner technologies and the eventual phasing out of fossil fuels.

Finally, you play a pivotal role in this transition. By staying informed, questioning the status quo, and demanding more from policymakers and companies, you can help steer our global community towards a more sustainable and just energy future. Remember, every discussion you initiate, every piece of information you share, and every action you take, no matter how small, contributes to a broader collective effort. Together, we can ensure that natural gas, our unsung hero, plays its part in our narrative without becoming the villain.

8

RETHINKING NUCLEAR ENERGY

"I was taught that the way of progress was neither swift nor easy."
- Marie Curie

Modern Nuclear Technologies

When you think about nuclear energy, what springs to mind? Perhaps it's giant cooling towers, complex machinery, or even concerns about safety. But let's dive into the modern era of nuclear technologies, where advancements are setting new benchmarks for safety, efficiency, and sustainability. Today, we're peeling back the layers on one of the most promising developments: the sodium-cooled Experimental Breeder Reactor-II (EBR-II).

Overview of Sodium-Cooled EBR-II

The EBR-II is not your everyday nuclear reactor. Unlike traditional water-cooled reactors, this technology leverages liquid sodium as a coolant. Why sodium, you ask? Sodium possesses excellent heat transfer capabilities and does not need to be pressurised like water, which significantly reduces the risk of coolant-related accidents.

Originally developed and tested in the United States during the mid-20th century, the EBR-II was designed not just to generate electricity, but also to demonstrate breeding and fuel reprocessing capabilities—turning waste into usable fuel. This reactor type represents a pivotal shift from reactors that simply consume fuel to those that can regenerate part of the fuel they use.

The core concept (pun intended) behind the EBR-II is its ability to operate at high temperatures but at atmospheric pressure, reducing the strain on the reactor vessel compared to water-cooled systems. This capability not only enhances safety but also improves the thermal efficiency of the power plant.

Safety Features

Diving deeper into the safety aspects, the sodium-cooled EBR-II introduces several innovative features that tackle the usual public apprehensions head-on. One of the standout safety features is its inherent passive safety system. In simpler terms, it means the reactor can shut down safely without human intervention or mechanical assistance in the event of an abnormal operational condition.

The use of liquid sodium eliminates the risks associated with high-pressure systems. In traditional reactors, the water used as coolant is under extreme pressure, and any breach could lead to significant steam releases or worse. Sodium, being a liquid metal, operates at atmospheric pressure, thus sidestepping the risks of pressurised steam explosions.

Moreover, the EBR-II was designed with a negative temperature coefficient of reactivity. This might sound a bit technical, but what it essentially means is that as the reactor heats up, its ability to sustain a nuclear chain reaction decreases. Therefore, if the reactor ever begins to overheat, the physics of how atoms interact within the core will naturally dampen the reaction, promoting self-regulation and preventing overheating.

Waste Recycling Capabilities

Now, let's talk about one of the most critical aspects of modern nuclear technologies: waste management. The traditional narrative surrounding nuclear energy often focuses on the long-lived radioactive waste it generates. However, the EBR-II flips this script by incorporating waste recycling capabilities.

The reactor is designed as a breeder, which means it generates more fissile material (the stuff that keeps the nuclear reaction going) than it consumes. How does it achieve this? By converting fertile material, like uranium-238 (which is abundant but not directly usable in most reactors), into plutonium-239, a fissile material. This process not only makes the EBR-II fuel-efficient but also reduces the amount of waste.

Additionally, the spent fuel from this reactor can be reprocessed and recycled. The reprocessing separates waste products from usable fuel materials, which can then be fabricated into new fuel rods. This cycle significantly cuts down on the volume and toxicity of the waste, addressing one of the major environmental concerns associated with nuclear power.

In embracing technologies like the EBR-II, the nuclear industry is making strides not only in advancing the efficiency and safety of nuclear power but also in ensuring its role as a sustainable and environmentally responsible energy source. As we continue to confront the challenges of climate change and the global need for clean energy, understanding and supporting advancements in technologies like sodium-cooled reactors could be key to unlocking a greener energy future.

So, as we rethink the role of nuclear energy in today's world, it's essential to keep an open mind about the potential of these modern technologies to address some of the most pressing issues facing our planet. With improved safety features, enhanced efficiency, and groundbreaking waste recycling capabilities, modern nuclear technologies like the EBR-II are reshaping perceptions and setting the stage for a sustainable power generation landscape.

Addressing Public Concerns

Debunking nuclear myths

When you hear the word "nuclear", does your mind instinctively picture mushroom clouds and disaster zones? You're not alone. Many of the fears surrounding nuclear energy are based on outdated information or extreme scenarios that don't reflect the reality of modern nuclear technology. Let's dismantle some of these myths.

The first myth is that nuclear power plants are accidents waiting to happen. The images of Chernobyl and Fukushima play into this fear, but these incidents, while serious, are exceptions rather than the rule. Advances in technology have significantly increased the safety of nuclear plants. Modern reactors, such as the sodium-cooled fast reactors, have passive safety systems that can shut down the plant automatically in case of an emergency without human intervention.

Another common myth is that nuclear power contributes to weapons proliferation. However, the technology used in power plants is quite different from that used in weapons. Furthermore, stringent international regulations and treaties are in place to prevent the spread of nuclear weapons technology.

Lastly, there's the belief that nuclear energy is bad for the environment. In reality, nuclear power is one of the cleanest sources of energy available today. It produces no air pollution or greenhouse gases during operation. The only byproduct, nuclear waste, is securely contained and managed under strict regulations.

Historical safety records

Now that we've tackled the myths, let's look at the facts. Historically, nuclear energy has been among the safest forms of electricity generation. According to the International Energy Agency, nuclear power causes fewer deaths per terawatt-hour produced than any other major source of power, including coal, oil, natural gas, and even hydroelectric power.

The safety of nuclear energy can be attributed to rigorous safety protocols and continuous improvements in reactor design. For instance, the EBR-II (Experimental Breeder Reactor-II), a prototype sodium-cooled reactor, operated safely for 30 years without any significant incident. It included multiple safety systems that could independently cool down the reactor without power or human intervention.

Moreover, the nuclear industry is highly regulated. Nuclear power plants are subject to strict oversight and regular inspections by national and international bodies to ensure they meet safety standards. These measures have helped to maintain an excellent safety record over the decades.

Comparative analysis with other energy sources

Comparing nuclear energy with other sources puts things into perspective. Let's consider coal, natural gas, and renewables like wind and solar.

Coal and natural gas plants emit large quantities of carbon dioxide and other pollutants that contribute to global warming and have detrimental health effects. In contrast, nuclear power plants produce no air pollution during operation. The waste they produce is contained and managed, not released into the environment.

On the renewables front, wind and solar are indeed crucial parts of our transition to a sustainable energy future. However, they have limitations, particularly in their variability and dependence on weather conditions. Nuclear energy, on the other hand, provides a stable and reliable base-load power. It can continuously generate large amounts of electricity regardless of weather conditions, making it an essential complement to intermittent renewable sources.

Regarding cost-effectiveness, initial construction costs of nuclear plants are high, but they are offset by the low operating costs and long lifespans of these plants. Nuclear reactors typically operate for40-60 years, and ongoing developments in technology may extend this lifespan even further.

Lastly, when considering long-term sustainability, nuclear energy stands out. With advancements in reactor design and the development of closed fuel cycles that recycle nuclear waste, the sustainability of nuclear energy continues to improve. The ability to reuse fuel not only decreases the amount of waste but also maximizes the energy extracted from the fuel.

In summary, when you weigh nuclear energy against other sources, its role as a safe, cost-effective, and sustainable energy source becomes clear. It's not a question of choosing between nuclear power and renewables but rather understanding how nuclear can complement other forms of energy to create a balanced and reliable energy supply. As we continue to combat climate change, embracing a realistic mix of energy sources, including nuclear, will be essential.

Nuclear in the Energy Mix

When you flip on a light switch, charge your phone, or boot up your computer, there's a good chance you're tapping into a power grid that's a mixed bag of energy sources. Solar farms, wind turbines, and yes, those controversial nuclear reactors all play a part. But let's zoom in on nuclear energy. Often seen as a pariah in the energy family, its role in baseload power generation, cost-effectiveness, and long-term sustainability might just sway your views.

Role in Baseload Power Generation

Understanding baseload power is key to getting why nuclear might not be the energy villain it's often made out to be. Baseload power is the minimum level of demand on an electrical grid over a span of time. Nuclear power excels here because it can provide large amounts of steady, uninterrupted electricity. Unlike solar or wind, which depend heavily on the weather, nuclear plants don't care if it's sunny or windy. They just keep on churning out power.

Now, you might wonder, how reliable is nuclear really? Picture this: a nuclear power plant has a capacity factor of around 92.5%. This means it's running at full clip more than 90% of the time. Wind turbines? They're at about 34.8%. Solar panels? Around 24.5%. These numbers aren't to criticize renewables — we need them in the mix! But they do highlight nuclear's stalwart role in keeping our grids stable and our lights on, no matter the weather.

Plus, with advancements in reactor technology, newer models can adjust output to better complement renewable sources. This flexibility helps to smooth out the energy supply and ensures that there's always enough power to meet demand, even when everyone's cranking their air conditioners on a scorching day.

Cost-effectiveness

Let's talk money, because ultimately, the cost is a massive factor in any energy debate. Initial setup costs for nuclear plants are steep, no sugarcoating here. Building a nuclear power plant requires a hefty investment in safety, regulation compliance, and technology. However, the plot thickens when you look at the operating costs over time.

Nuclear fuel costs are relatively low and stable. Consider the price volatility we see with fossil fuels — remember the last time oil prices spiked? Nuclear doesn't have that problem. Once the plant is up and running, the economics of nuclear power become more appealing. The levelised cost of electricity (LCOE) from nuclear remains competitive, particularly when you factor in the plant's long operational life — we're talking 60 years, even 80 with proper maintenance and upgrades. That's a long innings compared to other power sources.

Furthermore, with the push for carbon pricing and financial penalties on high-carbon energy production, nuclear's economic case might strengthen further. As policies shift towards penalising carbon emissions, nuclear energy stands out with its low-carbon credentials, potentially gaining an edge over costlier, carbon-heavy fossil fuels.

Long-term Sustainability

Here's where nuclear power plants really start to look like gems. Sustainability isn't just about keeping the lights on today; it's about ensuring we can do so tomorrow, next year, and next century without trashing the planet. Nuclear energy, with its low greenhouse gas emissions during operation, is a strong contender here.

Consider the entire lifecycle emissions of nuclear energy, including construction, operation, decommissioning, and waste disposal. Studies show that these are comparable to wind and much lower than coal and gas. This makes nuclear a critical player in our quest to slash global carbon emissions. In a world where reducing our carbon footprint is no longer optional but imperative, nuclear energy offers a substantial contribution to achieving those climate goals.

Moreover, nuclear waste, often spotlighted in discussions about sustainability, is being addressed through innovations in recycling and reprocessing technologies. These advancements not only help reduce the volume and toxicity of the waste but also improve the efficiency of resource use within the nuclear industry.

Yet, the sustainability of nuclear energy isn't solely about emissions or waste. It's also about how this energy source can coexist with renewables to provide a dependable, low-carbon energy grid. Integrating nuclear with renewable energies could create a robust system capable of powering our future while keeping carbon emissions in check.

In weaving nuclear into our broader energy tapestry, you can see how its attributes complement the intermittent nature of renewables. This synergy could be pivotal for a sustainable, stable, and cost-effective energy future.

So, as you consider the role of nuclear power in our energy mix, it's clear it has a card to play. It's not just about meeting today's energy demands but ensuring a resilient and sustainable system for the future. The question isn't really whether we can afford to include nuclear in our energy strategy, but whether we can afford not to.

RECAP AND ACTION ITEMS

We've delved deep into the potential of nuclear energy, unravelling the intricacies of modern technologies, addressing common public concerns, and evaluating its role in our future energy mix. By now, you've gained a clearer perspective on how advanced nuclear technologies, like the sodium-cooled EBR-II, are paving the way for safer and more sustainable energy production. These systems not only enhance safety with robust design features but also offer innovative solutions for waste recycling.

You've also walked through the fog of myths surrounding nuclear energy and emerged with factual, historical data that underlines its safety and efficiency compared to other energy sources. It's been an eye-opener to see how nuclear energy's track record stacks up against the rest, hasn't it?

Looking towards the future, recognising nuclear energy's role in providing reliable baseload power is crucial. Its cost-effectiveness and long-term sustainability make it a compelling component of a balanced energy strategy, aiming to meet global demands while curbing carbon emissions.

So, what can you do next? First, keep the conversation going. Talk about what you've learned with friends, family, or colleagues. Awareness and understanding are key steps towards acceptance and change.

Second, stay informed. The world of nuclear technology is rapidly evolving, and staying updated will help you make informed opinions and decisions about energy policies and personal energy choices.

Lastly, consider reaching out to your local representatives to express your support for including nuclear energy in the sustainable energy mix. Policies are influenced by public opinion, and your voice matters.

Remember, every big change starts with small, deliberate actions. By rethinking nuclear energy, you're not just considering an alternative power source—you're taking a step towards a cleaner, more sustainable future for all.

9

CLIMATE REPARATIONS AND GLOBAL INEQUALITY

"We cannot have climate justice without racial and economic justice." – Mary Robinson

The Concept of Climate Reparations

Diving headfirst into the deep blue sea of climate change discussions, one term that frequently washes ashore is "climate reparations." It's a concept that might tickle your curiosity or raise your eyebrows. Let's break it down together, shall we?

Origins and rationale

The idea of climate reparations is not just a new-age fad; it's steeped in the acknowledgment that historical and ongoing carbon emissions have disproportionately come from developed nations. Yet, the brunt of climate change impacts is borne by those least responsible for them—often poorer, developing countries. This imbalance sparked the debate on climate justice, advocating that those who have contributed most to the problem should assist those now facing its worst consequences.

Think of it as a kind of "polluter pays" principle. Developed nations industrialised early, reaping economic benefits and emitting vast amounts of greenhouse gases in the process. These gases, as you likely know, stick around in the atmosphere, warming the planet. Meanwhile, developing countries, with comparatively minimal contributions to these emissions, encounter severe challenges—think floods, droughts, and hurricanes. It's a global problem, but the scales of responsibility and impact are tipped unevenly.

The rationale behind climate reparations is about addressing these disparities. It's an ethical call to action to ensure that countries facing the existential threats of climate change receive support to mitigate these impacts and adapt to an increasingly hostile environment.

Current policy frameworks

You might wonder, "How does this all translate into action?" Various international frameworks have tried to tackle this issue, albeit with mixed success.

The United Nations Framework Convention on Climate Change (UNFCCC), including its landmark outcomes like the Kyoto

Protocol and the Paris Agreement, highlights principles of equity and common but differentiated responsibilities. These agreements recognise that richer countries should take the lead in combatting climate change and its effects.

Under the Paris Agreement, for instance, there's a commitment to mobilising $100 billion annually by 2020 from developed to developing countries. This fund is meant to help poorer nations cut emissions and strengthen resilience against climate impacts. However, achieving these funding goals has been, to put it mildly, a bumpy ride. Pledges don't always match payments, and when they do, the funds are often not enough or not efficiently allocated.

Another mechanism you might find intriguing is the concept of carbon credits. This approach allows countries or companies to buy and sell permits to emit carbon dioxide, ideally leading to an overall reduction in global emissions. However, the effectiveness and fairness of these markets are hotly debated. Critics argue that it allows rich countries to essentially pay their way out of genuine emission reductions, while supporters claim it's a pragmatic solution to a complex problem.

Impact assessments

So, what's the real-world impact of these climate reparations and policies? It's a mixed bag.

On the positive side, there have been tangible benefits in some regions. Funds from climate finance schemes have helped build renewable energy projects, improved water sanitation, and bolstered flood defenses in vulnerable communities. These initiatives not only combat climate change but also bring ancillary benefits like job creation and improved public health.

However, the effectiveness of climate reparations is often hampered by bureaucratic red tape, insufficient funding, and misalignment between the provided support and the actual needs of recipient countries. Assessments of climate finance impacts frequently point out that funds are too slow to come, too rigid in their usage stipulations, or too focused on short-term rather than sustainable, long-term benefits.

Moreover, there's the issue of whether these funds and projects genuinely constitute reparations or are merely aid dressed in another guise. True reparations would imply a transfer based not just on charity but on compensation for damages caused. This distinction is crucial but often blurred in international negotiations and national policies.

As you can see, the concept of climate reparations is fraught with complexities and controversies. It's not just about moving money but about moving towards a fairer and more equitable global framework for addressing climate change. As we continue to peel back the layers of this topic, keep these nuances in mind. Understanding the origins, frameworks, and impacts helps us gauge not just the effectiveness but the justice of our global response to climate change.

Consequences for Developing Nations

Dependency Culture

When you throw a lifeline to someone drowning, it's an act of heroism. But what if, instead of teaching them to swim, you just keep tossing out lifelines? This is a useful metaphor for understanding how climate reparation payments might inadvertently foster a dependency culture in developing nations. The aid is crucial, no doubt. It addresses immediate needs triggered by climate disasters which these countries, due to historical and economic disadvantages, are ill-equipped to handle alone. However, the continuous flow of aid can sometimes lead to a kind of reliance that's hard to break.

Imagine this: a country regularly receives funds to cope with the consequences of rising sea levels and increasingly ferocious weather patterns. These funds are vital for rebuilding and immediate relief but they do not always encourage or fund the infrastructure and policies needed for long-term resilience. The result? Each time a disaster strikes, these nations find themselves waiting for aid, rather than activating a robust, self-sufficient response mechanism.

Moreover, this dependency can shift focus from local governance and self-sustainability initiatives. Governments might find it easier to appeal for external funds rather than generating internal revenue or innovating local solutions. This can lead to a cycle where the primary energy is spent on securing the next tranche of aid, rather than developing a resilient economic and environmental strategy. The dependency culture thus undermines the very autonomy and resilience it aims to foster.

Stifling Economic Growth

You might think that a steady stream of financial aid would stimulate economic growth, but the reality can be quite different. Climate reparation funds are typically earmarked for immediate disaster response and rebuilding efforts. While crucial, these funds often sideline the broader economic development needed to lift countries out of poverty and vulnerability to climate impacts.

Consider a developing nation that receives substantial aid to restore areas devastated by a cyclone. The focus is on recovery — rebuilding homes, restoring power, and providing food and water. These are immediate needs that can't be ignored. However, this financial injection doesn't necessarily support businesses, enhance workforce skills, or develop industries. When funds are primarily defensive, they do little to advance the economy. What's more, if these funds are not managed transparently and effectively, they can lead to corruption and inefficiency, further throttling economic potential.

Economic development is sidelined not only by the nature of the funds but also by the message it sends to investors. The perception that a country is perpetually recovering from one disaster or another can deter private investment, which is often necessary for stimulating diverse economic growth. The narrative becomes one of eternal recovery rather than emerging opportunity, creating a challenging environment for sustainable growth and innovation.

Alternatives to Financial Aid

So, if relying heavily on financial aid isn't the panacea it appears to be, what alternatives should be considered? The key lies in solutions that not only address the immediate impacts of climate change but also empower nations to be self-sufficient in the long term.

One promising approach is investment in local capacity building. Instead of directing funds solely into disaster recovery, investing in education, healthcare, technology, and green industries could provide the tools these nations need to build a sustainable future. For instance, training local communities in sustainable agricultural techniques can reduce dependence on aid while ensuring food security.

Another alternative is facilitating technology transfer. Developed nations can assist by sharing technology that helps monitor weather patterns, improve crop yields, or generate renewable energy. This kind of support goes beyond temporary relief and lays the groundwork for enduring resilience.

Lastly, encouraging public-private partnerships can drive economic growth while addressing climate challenges. These partnerships can mobilise capital for large-scale infrastructure projects like water management systems or renewable energy installations, which not only help in adapting to climate impacts but also create jobs and stimulate local economies.

In shifting the focus from dependency to development, from temporary relief to sustainable growth, we empower developing nations not just to survive the next disaster, but to thrive in the face of ongoing challenges. This approach fosters a resilience that is self-sustaining, breaking the cycle of dependency and paving the way for a future that is robust, vibrant, and self-reliant.

Crafting Better Policies

Ensuring fairness and effectiveness

When you delve into the complexities of climate policy, fairness and effectiveness often stand at opposite corners, waiting to be reconciled. The challenge is crafting policies that not only address the massive scope of climate change but also distribute responsibilities and benefits fairly across all nations, especially between developed and developing countries.

Firstly, consider the principle of 'common but differentiated responsibilities' recognised in international climate agreements. It acknowledges that while all nations are in this together, not all hold the same culpability or capacity. A fair policy should account for historical emissions, current capabilities, and future potential. For instance, policies might require more from countries that have historically contributed more to carbon emissions. But how do you keep this fair? By coupling these demands with technical and financial support, ensuring that all countries can meet their targets without sacrificing their developmental goals.

Moreover, effectiveness hinges on clear, achievable goals and robust monitoring systems. You wouldn't bake a cake without checking if your oven works, right? Similarly, international commitments need to be backed by transparent reporting and verification methods to ensure everyone sticks to their part of the deal. This not only helps in tracking progress but also in building trust among nations—a crucial ingredient in international relations.

Building resilience and sustainability

Moving to the second part, building resilience and sustainability, you dive into the heart of what makes societies last. It's all about reducing vulnerability to climate impacts and ensuring that development doesn't come at the expense of the environment. Think of it as setting up a business: you wouldn't pour your resources into a venture that's likely to collapse with the first market fluctuation.

For developing countries, this is particularly crucial. Climate change hits them hardest, not just because of geographical and economic factors, but due to weaker infrastructure. Building resilience means integrating climate risk assessments into all facets of planning and development. From constructing flood-resistant buildings to diversifying crops to withstand drought, strategies need to be tailored to local needs and capacities.

Sustainability also means looking beyond immediate fixes and considering long-term impacts. Policies should promote sustainable practices such as renewable energy, efficient water use, and waste reduction. These practices not only mitigate the effects of climate change but also help in conserving resources for future generations. It's about making sure that while we meet today's needs, we aren't stealing from tomorrow's supplies.

Encouraging innovation and self-reliance

The final piece of the policy puzzle is fostering innovation and self-reliance. This is where you ignite the spark of creativity to tackle climate change. Innovation in this context isn't just about new gadgets and gizmos; it's about innovative ways of thinking, governing, and doing business that align with ecological boundaries.

Self-reliance is particularly potent. It empowers communities, making them less dependent on external aid and more capable of crafting their own, tailored responses to climate challenges. For example, local renewable energy projects can reduce reliance on imported oil, keep the air cleaner, and keep the economy booster running. Similarly, local food production systems can reduce the carbon footprint of imported groceries and bolster food security.

Policies should encourage such initiatives by providing the necessary legal and financial frameworks. This could mean offering tax incentives for green businesses, or streamlining regulations to make it easier for new technologies to reach the market. Furthermore, education plays a pivotal role. By embedding sustainability and climate science in educational curriculums, we cultivate a generation equipped to deal with and innovate for the world's looming climate challenges.

In crafting these policies, think of them as tools in a toolkit. Just as a carpenter wouldn't use a hammer to saw a board, policymakers must pick the right tool for the job, considering the specific needs and contexts of different regions. Fairness, resilience, sustainability, and innovation are not just lofty ideals; they are practical necessities for crafting policies that are as effective as they are equitable. By focusing on these areas, you're not just patching up today's problems but are laying down the groundwork for a healthier, more sustainable future.

RECAP AND ACTION ITEMS

As we unravel the layers of climate reparations and global inequality, it's clear that addressing the past and current impacts of climate change is not just about financial aid—it's about reshaping policies to create a fairer, more resilient world. The concept of climate reparations hinges on accountability and the need to compensate those who are disproportionately affected by environmental changes they had little hand in creating. Yet, as we've explored, the implementation of these policies must be meticulously crafted to avoid fostering a dependency culture or inadvertently stifling economic growth in developing nations.

Certainly, the journey towards effective climate justice is complex, involving a delicate balance between supporting those in need and empowering them to forge their own path to sustainability. This means going beyond mere monetary handouts to fostering environments where innovation and self-reliance can flourish.

Here's what you can do to contribute to this cause:

1. Educate Yourself and Others: Knowledge is power. Continue to inform yourself about the nuances of climate policies and their impacts. Share this knowledge to raise awareness and fuel informed debates that can lead to better solutions.

2. Advocate for Fair Policies: Engage with your local and national representatives to push for policies that not only aim to repair but also rebuild. Policies should be transparent, considering the socio-economic realities of those most affected by climate change.

3. Support Sustainable Practices: Whether it's choosing to buy from companies that have robust environmental policies or supporting local initiatives that aim to build resilience in vulnerable communities, your choices make a difference.

4. Encourage Innovation: Innovation isn't just for the tech industry. Supporting grassroots innovations in renewable energy or sustainable agriculture can transform communities. Look for opportunities to invest in or promote innovative solutions that address climate change.

5. Stay Involved: The fight against climate change and the quest for justice are ongoing. Stay engaged through forums, discussions, and networks that focus on creating sustainable and fair climate policies.

By taking these steps, you're not just a bystander but an active participant in shaping a more equitable and sustainable future. Remember, every action counts in the global effort to ensure that our responses to climate change are as just as they are effective.

10

TAKING ACTION: PRACTICAL STEPS FOR THE SCEPTICAL

"Never doubt that a small group of thoughtful, committed citizens can change the world; indeed, it's the only thing that ever has." - Margaret Mead

Individual Impact

Let's dive straight into the heart of the matter: what can you, as an individual, realistically do to combat climate change? With a deluge of information and often conflicting advice, it's easy to feel like a small cog in a vast environmental machine. However, the truth is, your actions possess a unique power to influence not just your immediate environment, but also the broader narrative on climate change.

Realistic Actions Individuals Can Take

First things first, let's cut through the noise and focus on actionable, effective strategies that slot neatly into your daily routine without demanding radical lifestyle changes. Here are a few pragmatic steps to consider:

1. Reduce Energy Use at Home: This isn't about sitting in the dark but making smarter choices. Switch to LED bulbs, unplug devices when not in use, and consider energy-efficient appliances. Even better, if possible, invest in smart home technologies that help monitor and manage your energy usage more effectively.

2. Revamp Your Travel Habits: Think about how you commute. Can you carpool, cycle, or use public transport? Perhaps not every day, but even a small reduction in your weekly car usage can have a significant impact. For longer distances, consider trains over planes where feasible, and when driving is the only option, ensure your vehicle is well-maintained to optimise fuel efficiency.

3. Mindful Eating: The food industry is a major greenhouse gas emitter, particularly meat and dairy production. You don't have to go vegan overnight, but even one plant-based meal a week can make a difference. Also, focus on local and seasonal produce to cut down on food miles.

4. Waste Not, Want Not: Reduce, reuse, and recycle should be your mantra. Minimise your waste by choosing products with less packaging, reusing items wherever possible, and recycling

correctly. Composting organic waste is another step forward in reducing methane emissions from landfills.

Debunking Myths about Personal Carbon Footprints

Despite the clear benefits of the actions mentioned, there's a persistent myth that individual choices don't matter in the grand scheme of things. Let's debunk this:

- Myth: "My actions are just a drop in the ocean." Reality: Oceans are made up of drops. Each action you take influences others around you, creates demand for greener products, and sets norms that businesses and governments can't ignore

- Myth: "Switching off my light doesn't matter if industries continue polluting." Reality: Demand drives supply. Reducing your energy consumption contributes to a decrease in overall energy demand, which in turn influences energy production strategies and policies.

- Myth: "Recycling doesn't matter; everything ends up in a landfill anyway." Reality: While not all recycled materials avoid landfills, proper recycling significantly reduces the waste that does. Plus, it conserves resources and energy.

How to Make a Real Difference Without Falling Prey to Tokenism

Tokenism in environmental actions often stems from well-intentioned but poorly informed decisions. Here's how to ensure your actions are impactful and not just for show:

- Educate Yourself: Stay informed about the most pressing environmental issues and understand where you can have the most impact. Resources like the IPCC reports, reputable environmental news sources, and academic journals are great places to start.

- Be Consistent and Persistent: Real change is a marathon, not a sprint. Integrate sustainable practices into your life that you can maintain long-term rather than adopting sweeping changes that are unsustainable for you personally.

- Support Structural Changes: While individual actions are crucial, supporting systemic changes can amplify your impact. Advocate for policies that promote renewable energy, conservation efforts, and green technologies.

- Accountability and Transparency: When engaging in environmental actions, hold yourself accountable. Track your carbon footprint using online calculators and set personal goals. Be transparent with others about your journey, sharing both successes and areas for improvement, which can inspire similar actions.

In essence, remember that your individual impact is not just about reducing emissions or conserving water; it's about setting a precedent, influencing others, and contributing to a larger cultural shift towards sustainability. Your everyday choices do matter, and they ripple outwards in ways you might not immediately see but are nonetheless vital in the collective fight against climate change.

Community Initiatives

Examples of Effective Community-Led Environmental Actions

Let's dive right into the heart of community action. Imagine your local area bustling not just with people and traffic but with initiatives that directly benefit the environment. It's happening around the globe, and it can happen in your community too.

Take the example of the Incredible Edible project in Todmorden, England. Residents of this small town began growing fruit, herbs, and vegetables around their town—on unused land, along railway tracks, and outside police stations. Not only did this initiative beautify the area, but it also provided free, fresh produce to residents and passersby, fostering a strong sense of community while subtly promoting sustainability.

In urban settings, community gardens are a powerful tool for green action. These gardens not only provide local, fresh produce but also help to improve urban air quality and promote biodiversity. For instance, the city of Detroit, once struggling with economic decline, has seen a transformation in several areas, becoming lush with over 1,400 gardens and farms spread across the city. These initiatives help combat food scarcity, engage community members, and repurpose vacant urban land into thriving green spaces.

Transition Towns provide another compelling model. Originating from Totnes, England, this movement empowers communities to address the ecological and economic crises stemming from the overuse of fossil fuels. Each Transition Town builds local resilience through efforts like renewable energy projects, local currency systems, and sustainable transport schemes, all driven by what the locals decide is most needed in their area.

How to Organise and Mobilise at the Local Level

Organising your community around environmental issues might seem daunting, but it's all about starting small and thinking big. The first step is often the simplest: start talking. Hold a meeting at a local community centre or even in your living room. Invite neighbours, friends, and local experts. Discuss what environmental issues are most pressing in your area. Is it waste management, the loss of green spaces, or perhaps air quality? A focused discussion can spark ideas and forge initial connections.

Next, harness the power of social media. Platforms like Facebook, Twitter, and Instagram can amplify your message and reach a broader audience. Create a group or hashtag for your initiative to gather community input and share progress. This digital presence can be a rallying point, a place to organise logistics, and a tool to attract more volunteers.

Remember, every significant movement begins with a single step. The city of Hamburg, Germany, for instance, decided to make public transport free on days when air pollution reached critical levels. This small start led to broader discussions and actions aimed at reducing reliance on personal vehicles, spurred initially by just a few concerned citizens and local advocacy groups.

Building Coalitions for Broader Impact

While starting local is key, the real magic happens when local efforts inspire and connect with wider networks. Building coalitions can amplify your impact, bringing in diverse skills and resources and spreading successful strategies across wider areas.

One effective approach is partnering with local businesses. Many companies are eager to enhance their corporate responsibility credentials and can provide resources, whether it's funding, space, or expertise. Local schools and universities are also great allies. They can involve students in projects, integrate environmental action into their curricula, and bring academic expertise to your initiatives.

Moreover, look to join forces with existing environmental groups and NGOs. These organisations often have a wealth of experience in policy, advocacy, and community organising. They can offer guidance and support, help navigate legal and bureaucratic hurdles, and connect you with a broader network of activists.

Take inspiration from the Plastic Free July movement, which started in Western Australia and has grown into a global phenomenon. By aligning with businesses, schools, and other organisations, they've massively extended their reach, helping millions of people become more aware of their plastic use and reducing global plastic pollution significantly.

In all these efforts, the key is to maintain open communication, align your goals, and ensure that every participant feels valued and heard. Building a coalition is not about leading alone; it's about walking together.

Through these steps, your community can become a beacon of environmental action, inspiring others and making a tangible impact on the planet. Whether it's through creating green spaces, organising sustainability workshops, or advocating for policy changes, remember that every small action contributes to a larger change. By mobilising your community, you are not only working towards a sustainable environment but also building a more connected, proactive, and aware society.

Policy Advocacy

Engaging with and influencing policymakers might sound like a task reserved for seasoned lobbyists or those with insider connections. However, in the realm of climate advocacy, every voice truly counts, and there are effective ways for you to make yours heard. The key is understanding the mechanics of political engagement and using them to your advantage.

How to Engage with and Influence Policy Makers

First things first: know who you're trying to influence. This isn't just about recognising faces on the news—it's about understanding who holds the reins on environmental policies in your area. Are they local councillors, state legislators, or national representatives? Once you've pinpointed the relevant players, it's time to get their attention.

One of the most direct approaches is to establish communication. This could be through emails, phone calls, or even attending town hall meetings. When you communicate, be clear and concise about what you want—whether it's stricter emissions regulations, support for renewable energy projects, or anything else climate-related. Be specific about the issue and what action you propose. Remember, clarity is persuasive.

However, don't just stop at digital or telephonic outreach. Personal letters or scheduled meetings can make an even stronger impact. In these interactions, sharing personal stories about how climate change affects you and your community can be particularly powerful. Stories resonate more deeply than statistics alone, as they humanise the issues.

Another effective method is participating in public consultations. These are often held when new policies are being considered. By voicing your opinions here, you provide direct input into the legislative process. It's democracy in action—make sure you're a part of it.

Crafting Messages that Resonate with Politicians and the Public

Crafting a message that resonates requires you to speak both to the head and the heart. You need to balance factual data with emotional appeal. Politicians care about data, but they also care about stories from their constituents that can be retold, stories that humanise the dry stats and figures.

When putting together your message, focus on the impact of climate change that everyone can understand and relate to, such as health issues, security, and economic benefits. For instance, emphasising the health implications of poor air quality can engage a broader audience than complex discussions on carbon trading might.

Use simple, jargon-free language. Remember, you're not just talking to experts in environmental science; you're speaking to laypeople and decision-makers who might not have a background in the field. The simpler your message, the broader its reach and impact.

Moreover, tailor your messages for different platforms. What works in a face-to-face meeting might not resonate on social media, and vice versa. On social platforms, visuals and brief, impactful messages often work best. For more formal proposals, detailed reports and case studies are more appropriate.

Strategies for Effective Environmental Advocacy

Effective advocacy is as much about building alliances as it is about having compelling arguments. Start by joining or forming networks of like-minded individuals. There's strength in numbers, and a group can often get meetings and attention that individuals cannot.

Next, leverage the power of the media. Write op-eds, participate in interviews, or use social media platforms to amplify your message. Media coverage not only puts pressure on policymakers but also raises public awareness, which in turn increases public pressure on those policymakers.

Don't forget the importance of continuous engagement. Policymaking is rarely a quick process. Stay informed about progress and keep in touch with policymakers and their staff. Offer yourself as a resource they can turn to for information on environmental issues. This helps build a relationship of trust and establishes you as a credible voice on the matter.

Finally, always be prepared to offer solutions, not just criticism. Policymakers are more likely to engage with constructive suggestions that come with clear, actionable steps. Whether you're proposing a new policy, a modification to an existing one, or an entirely new project, make sure you present it as a well-thought-out solution that addresses potential counterarguments.

In summary, while the realm of policy advocacy might initially seem daunting, breaking it down into manageable actions can make it an incredibly effective tool in your climate action arsenal. By understanding how to engage with policymakers, crafting resonant messages, and employing strategic advocacy techniques, you can play a pivotal role in shaping the policies that will determine our environmental future.

RECAP AND ACTION ITEMS

By now, you've got a solid foundation in understanding how you, as an individual, can make a meaningful impact on climate change. You've sifted through the myths and know that your personal carbon footprint isn't just a drop in the ocean. It's a vital piece of the larger puzzle. Remember, realistic actions like reducing waste, improving energy efficiency at home, and choosing sustainable transport options are not just good on paper; they are impactful when implemented consistently.

Turning to your community, the potential for collective action is enormous. You've seen examples of community-led initiatives that have not only improved local environments but also set a precedent for others to follow. It's about harnessing that collective energy and turning it into something tangible. Start by engaging with your community—whether it's through organising clean-up drives, promoting local sustainability projects, or advocating for green policies at community meetings.

When it comes to policy advocacy, remember that your voice is powerful. Engaging with policymakers, crafting compelling messages, and employing strategic advocacy are not just for the seasoned activists; they are tools available to you. By clearly communicating the urgency and providing viable solutions, you can influence policy and contribute to broader environmental change.

Now, what next? Here are some concrete steps you can take:

1. Audit Your Lifestyle: Identify areas where you can reduce your carbon footprint. Start small, perhaps with reducing energy usage or cutting down on single-use plastics.

2. Educate Yourself and Others: The more you know, the better equipped you are to make informed decisions and persuade others. Share what you learn, host informational sessions, or start a blog.

3. Connect with Local Groups: There's strength in numbers. Join environmental groups in your area or start your own. The more connected you are, the bigger the impact you can make.

4. Reach Out to Representatives: Don't underestimate the power of communication. Write to your local representatives about environmental issues that concern you and push for change.

5. Stay Consistent and Patient: Change doesn't happen overnight. Stay committed to your actions, keep learning, and keep pushing for change, both locally and beyond.

Every step you take builds a path towards a more sustainable and equitable planet. Your actions, your voice, and your commitment can drive change. Let's make it count.

THE FUTURE IS YOURS TO SHAPE

As we draw the curtains on this explorative journey, it is essential to step back and ponder the profound implications of the insights you've gathered. The environmental landscape is intricate and ever-evolving, with myriad factors intertwined in a delicate balance. The understanding you now hold is not just a beacon in the murk but a call to wield your knowledge with intention and action.

The impact of human activity on our planet is undeniable, and the choices we make today shape the world of tomorrow. It's crucial to recognise that each decision, no matter how small, contributes to a larger environmental outcome. Whether it's the energy sources we support, the products we consume, or the policies we advocate for, every action counts.

You are armed now with a deeper understanding of the complexities surrounding conventional and renewable energy resources. This knowledge bestows upon you the power to influence not only your personal choices but also the broader societal approach towards sustainable practices. The transition towards renewable energy, despite its challenges and "dark sides," is an essential step towards reducing our ecological footprint and fostering a sustainable future.

However, embracing renewables is not merely about adopting new technologies but also about cultivating a mindset of sustainability and resilience. It is about understanding the limitations and potential of these technologies and striving for a balanced approach that considers environmental, economic, and social factors. You are called upon to be an advocate for change, to challenge the status quo, and to inspire others to join in the movement towards a more sustainable world.

Moreover, the dependence on conventional energy is a complex issue that requires more than just a switch to alternative sources. It entails a comprehensive re-evaluation of our energy policies, economic models, and societal values. It's about creating systems that not only meet our current needs without compromising the ability of future generations to meet theirs but also respect the natural boundaries of our planet.

As you move forward, remember that the journey towards sustainability is a collaborative endeavour. It requires the collective efforts of individuals, communities, governments, and international bodies. Your role in this collective effort is crucial. You have the capacity to initiate conversations, influence policy, and implement sustainable practices in your community and beyond.

Now, imagine a future where sustainable practices are the norm, where renewable energy powers our lives, and where economic growth does not come at the expense of our planet. This future is not just a dream but a possibility that is within your reach. It requires courage, commitment, and creativity—qualities that you possess.

To make this vision a reality, continuous learning and adaptation are essential. Stay informed about the latest developments in technology, policy, and practice. Engage with experts, join environmental groups, and participate in forums that foster dialogue and action on sustainability issues. Your ongoing engagement is vital in driving the momentum towards a sustainable future.

If the insights from this exploration have sparked a desire in you to delve deeper or if you seek to implement transformative changes in your personal life or within your organisation, professional guidance can amplify your impact. Whether it's developing sustainable business strategies, enhancing your home's energy efficiency, or advocating for policy changes, expert advice can provide you with the tools and confidence to make informed decisions and take effective action.

In conclusion, the path ahead is replete with challenges but also rich with opportunity. You are equipped not only with knowledge but with the power to effect change. Embrace this role with enthusiasm and determination. The actions you take today will resonate beyond your immediate environment, contributing to a legacy of sustainability and resilience.

The future is not predetermined. It is shaped by the choices we make now. So, make choices that you can look back on with pride—choices that demonstrate care for the planet and for future generations. Let this be your call to action. Let's build a future that is sustainable, equitable, and thriving for all.

Take your next step today.

Printed in Great Britain
by Amazon